REBUILDING WHAT WAS DESTROYED

REBUILDING

WHAT WAS

DESTROYED

How A Mother's Bold Faith
Changed Everything

SIONI RODRIGUEZ & SCHEILA SINGLEY

ISBN 1-65619-149-0
ISBN-13 978-1-65619-149-6

We have recreated events, locales, and conversations
from our memories of them. To maintain their
anonymity, we have changed some names of individuals
and places. We have changed some identifying
characteristics and details such as physical properties, and
places of residence.

Scriptures taken from the Holy Bible, New
International Version®, NIV®. Copyright © 1973,
1978, 1984, 2011 by Biblica, Inc.™ Used by permission
of Zondervan. All rights reserved worldwide.
www.zondervan.com The "NIV" and "New
International Version" are trademarks registered in the
United States Patent and Trademark Office by
Biblica, Inc.™

writer-editor: Jane Fisher
www.janefisheronline.com

Printed in the United States of America

Available for purchase at Amazon.com

DEDICATION

To Jesus, our Lord and Savior, and source of all
our strength.

To our family, who has supported us as we
advocate for this cause.

To all those women, whether behind bars or free,
waiting for their second chance.

To the prayer warriors who pull souls out of the
fire and mediate for those who are lost and starved
for the truth.

And to the fiercest warriors walking the earth who
have stepped up to answer the call to spread the
gospel in the darkest places.

"For I know the plans I have for you," declares the Lord, *"plans to prosper you and not to harm you, plans to give you hope and a future. Then you will call on me and come and pray to me, and I will listen to you. You will seek me and find me when you seek me with all your heart."*

Jeremiah 29:11-13 New International Version (NIV)

CONTENTS

FOREWORD

We don't often hear about women in prison. From time to time, the news will carry a story of a popular celebrity who ends up in a "white collar prison." Then there are those low-budget movies that show a sensationalized version of life behind bars. Neither of these shows a realistic view of life for a woman who is incarcerated. It's easier not to think about it at all. And most of us don't. No wonder these women feel like they must've been forgotten by everyone.

But Sioni doesn't forget. She and her husband, Richard, have been volunteers in the prison ministry of their church for years. They bring the Word of God to the incarcerated, three Sundays each month. They do this without passing judgment on the inmates. They do this because their faith in God has led them to this cause. They do this because someone else did it for Sioni's daughter, Scheila.

This story is told from two perspectives. Scheila tells about her experience being in prison and how it affected the rest of her life. Sioni put her faith to the test, convinced that God had a plan and purpose for her daughter. Her trust proved to be well-placed, and now she has made it her life's purpose to spread that hope to others. Her passion is to spread the word that God has a plan and purpose for each of us, and that He's always ready to give us another chance to get life right.

Scheila is now a wife and mother, has attended seminary and has received her master's degree in theology. Sioni serves women who are currently in prison, to encourage them and to bring hope to those who need it the most. They both have a deep love of God, each other, and the people whose lives they touch.

There are many ways that Sioni shows how much she cares about the women she reaches out to. One of them is a habit that immediately demonstrates her interest in their well-being. At the start of each class, she goes around the table and asks each of the inmates the same question. "On a scale of 1 to 10, with 10 being the best, how would you rate the kind of day you're having today?"

The crucial step is that after asking, she listens intently to each woman's answer.

As a way of honoring this, the stories in each chapter develop on that 1-to-10 scale. The early chapters may seem bleak and despondent. But by the time you reach chapter 10, you will have seen growth and will discover stories of some of their best days.

This book provides a glimpse of life in prison—from both sides of the cell door. I will forever treasure the opportunity, now shared with you, to hear each of them tell of their experiences.

—*Jane Fisher, January 2020*

REBUILDING WHAT WAS DESTROYED

INTRODUCTION

Sioni

As I walked down the cold, gray hall toward the correctional officer, I realized that I wasn't the least bit nervous. This was my first time visiting a prison ward. Beyond that, this was a maximum security facility. I should have been at least anxious. Instead, I felt energized, eager and excited.

A huge glass wall at the front of the unit came into view ahead. Through it, I could see the inmates dressed in red jumpsuits. Red happens to be my favorite color. To me, when I saw them all in red, I thought they looked beautiful! I smiled to myself. This is a very good sign!

I didn't know at the time that the correctional officer was as new as I was. Neither of us was exactly familiar with the procedure for my visit. I approached, unable to tell from his demeanor what he expected from me. I decided to keep it simple.

"I'm here to conduct a bible study group in the maximum security area."

He directed me towards a door. "It's there. Go ahead."

It wasn't until later that I found out I shouldn't have been allowed to go inside the glass and into the cell block. I was actually supposed to go to a room that was right beside the officer, where the women would come to me for our class. There, the officer could keep the inmates I was here to see—and me—under closer supervision.

But he passed me through without another word. I struggled to open the heavy, blue door, and I found myself inside the glass room.

There seemed to be nothing, in particular, happening. There were several conversations going on at the same time. Some women were warming food in the microwave. Others were walking around outside their cells.

The room got very still as I walked in. All eyes turned in my direction. I must admit that, at that point, I felt a little like Daniel in the Lion's Den!

New to this and not really knowing how to open the conversation, I said, in my most cheerful voice, "Hey Girls!"

That was met with dead silence.

They looked at me as if to say, "What the heck are you doing in here?"

I felt completely deflated and totally at a loss. But I kept going. I was committed now, and I stuck with it.

"Anyone want to have some girl talk?"

Several women gave me a hard look and went back inside their cells. But some of them hung around to see what would happen. After a while, they started to warm up to me.

That day, I learned a lesson that would serve me well in all my visits to come.

Just a little talking, a little listening, a little caring, goes a long, long way.

I continue to go back to see them. When they see me coming from the other side of the glass, they wave and are excited to see me.

And I still find them beautiful.

PRELUDE

Scheila

It was about three o'clock in the morning. The other inmates were sleeping in their cells. They stuck me in a cell with an older black woman. She must have been in her 50s. I could tell she was a veteran of the system.

I remember crying when I got into the cell. I wasn't loud. I tried to be as quiet as I could, but it was hard to contain my sniffles. I remember my cellmate as she got out of her bunk.

I was lying on the top bunk. When you come in and you're a newbie—*fresh meat*—you never get a bottom bunk. All the bottom bunks are usually taken because it's easier for people to get on and off the lower bunk.

"Shhh."

The first thing that anyone said to me when I got there. This woman got up close to my bunk and said, "Shhh." There was no sweetness, no *Mommy's here. Everything's going to be okay.*

"You'd better stop that crying because they're going to devour you alive. Get it together. Get it out and get it out good. Don't let them see you cry."

And that was my introduction to what I was about to face.

⌘

My first emotion when I realized I was going to prison was fear, quickly followed by despair. After that came hopelessness, then anger. I thought this was the way it would be from then on. I had to go through all these steps until I recognized that it was all part of the grieving process. Eventually, for me, the last step was my reformation. But there is a lot to tell before we get there.

" 1 "

I FEEL COLD

There are about 20 cells on two floors. It's a big pod, with rows of doors lining each side. Walking into the room, I see several tables, and a TV hanging in one of the corners.

All those doors open up and that's where I go inside if it's a lockdown time or sleep time. Mine is a two-person cell on the lower floor, two doors in. Not much inside these cells other than two bunks, a desk, and a little toilet there "for your comfort."

There's a routine, and every day is the same. When it's time to go to bed, the doors will close. They won't open again until breakfast. Breakfast call is usually around 6 or 7 in the morning. First, the lights come on. Next, I hear the automatic click. It's a loud, metallic click. It signals that the locks are open, and we can come out for breakfast.

We're confined to a very small area. Depending on the level of security you're in, there's more or less freedom. In this county jail, I'm in the pod, all day and all night. Downtime is when we can relax outside of our cell in the dayroom.

We're allowed out in the dayroom until about noon. At noon, I go back inside my cell. The correctional officers (CO's) come through and they take a count. We stay in our cells for around two hours while there's a shift change, or whatever they have to do. Then we come back out and have lunch. Trustees—the inmates who help in the pod—bring the food in on trays.

After lunch, we get to relax for a little while again. The tables in the common room are used for everything. We play cards; some people read their books, do their puzzles. The community room is the only thing we share with everybody. We like to call it our living room.

Eventually, we're sent back to our cells for an hour or two lock-down. When I come back out, I eat dinner and spend the rest of the night outside the cell until it's time to go to bed.

During certain days of the week, a CO takes me outside for some recreational time. It's not actually outside. It's just another room, with a window if I'm lucky. Or another room with a wall where I can bounce a ball that they've given me. Or they have some meetings—AA meetings or NA meetings. Or sometimes they have religious studies where a nun or a priest comes in.

Certain chaplains come in. They might have little Bible studies, although studies are usually AA or NA meetings. They tend to go hand in hand. There's no actual church service. AA or NA meetings are supposed to take the place of spiritual guidance.

That was my schedule for most days unless I was in solitary. Sometimes I was in solitary for fighting. There was a time when I did two months straight in solitary confinement. That's 23 hours of lock-down and an hour out of the cell. It's in a whole different section that's isolated from where the main population is.

While I was first incarcerated, nobody came in to teach about Jesus. That wasn't how it worked. Nobody was coming to visit us. The chaplain was there if we wanted to talk, but nobody would come to teach us about the Word of God.

Sioni

First, there's this huge room, with tables everywhere, and that's the common room. Past the common room is a separate space, and that's the room where we do our class. When I walk in, the girls who are cleaning start setting up the table. They have plastic chairs, and everyone grabs one. I start to get my own chair, but one of them always says, "No, no! I'll get your chair!"

Sometimes we sing together. They have a radio, but it's so old that I can never get it to work. Still, the girls have tried to fix it for me.

I begin sitting down, but that doesn't usually last long. I like to walk around, and I use my hands a lot when I'm leading a group. When I want to connect more closely, I'll sit down again so that I can more easily make eye contact with them.

I might repeat myself a couple of times if they look confused. Because of my Spanish accent, I want to make sure they understand what I'm saying. Even without my accent, understanding the lesson could be difficult. These women, who feel so unlovable, might be hearing this message for the first time. The message? There's hope because the Creator of the universe loves you!

Sometimes I use a prop to illustrate what I'm teaching. I might toss a plastic cup and have one of them catch it—or not catch it. I'll use this to illustrate how God can intervene in our lives.

"That's how God sees us, sometimes. God is waiting there to catch us. But a lot of times we fall. We break into pieces. Then God comes along and

He pulls us all together again, and He makes us whole."

Scheila

It was one of the saddest, loneliest days that I had to endure in a long time. It wasn't my first fist fight ever, but it was the first one in jail. This was different. I remember every detail.

Our pod was considered the "serious offender" pod. It was for women who were coming into the county jail for crimes that were violent. Crimes like assaults, rapes, murders, drive-by shootings. Anything that had to do with a victim.

I remember one day, in particular. A young Mexican woman named Carmen arrived at the pod, and she did not speak any English. But God had gifted me with the ability to speak Spanish. My parents had taught me, so I was able to communicate with her. We formed a relationship.

Carmen was the mother of two children—a son, and a daughter. She was happily married. Her husband was a construction worker who owned a home that was in a very nice area, and not too far from the county jail. I asked her what had happened, what she was being locked up for. That seemed to be a prime topic in jail. Everybody wants to know what you're locked up for. It's as if you want to read a person by what crime was committed because your crime says a lot about you.

She explained to me that she was pulled over for driving without a license. The bigger problem was that Carmen did not understand the officer's orders. Her children were in the car when she was detained. When an officer had tried to put her in his car, she fought him.

She had gotten a charge of obstruction and evading the police. She tried to get away because her children were in her car. On top of all that, she was undocumented. She knew she was pulled over because the officer ran the plates. He hadn't called a traffic infraction or anything. He ran the plates, and it pulled up that the owner's registration was suspended.

The registrar was her husband, and it was his car. They asked for her paperwork, and it was then that they found out that she was in this country illegally. At that point, they detained her for all these crimes. Carmen would be held until eventually, ICE would come to pick her up.

When she came in, she was frantic. She had never been arrested before. She had never been in the position she was in, and she was hysterical thinking of her children. I asked the CO if they could place her in the cell next to me because she couldn't speak English. In the cell next to me, one of the girls had just left the floor, so I knew that one of the beds was open. The CO was kind enough to let her move in there.

A couple of weeks went by, and a new inmate came into the pod. She was a biker woman named Tanya. She must have been in her mid-thirties, but she had no children, and she was not married. She was tall, heavy-set and tough. And she was addicted to methamphetamines. She was in jail for assault, after beating a girl half to death when she was high.

One day, Carmen came to me, and she was extremely distraught. She told me that Tanya was hitting her with her food tray every morning. Sometimes I would sleep in for breakfast or my cellmate and I would eat together on the desk in our cell. This made it so that I hadn't seen it happen. The next morning, I made it a point to come to breakfast.

I've got to see this with my own eyes. If this is going on, I've got to defend her.

It's a kind of honor code. You look out for your cellie. You look out for your people.

I know that people might think, was this a race thing? But no, it wasn't because Carmen was Hispanic and the woman who assaulted her was white. That's not what the case was here. It was that the woman was assaulting her. No matter what her race was, I would have reacted the same way. Carmen and I had formed a relationship while we were incarcerated. She became almost like an aunt to me.

Sioni

I remember a beautiful young girl. She was sent to prison for drugs. She was charged with prostitution, but she was actually a victim of human trafficking. She came from England to the United States to someone who sold her. She came to the class, but she didn't participate. She explained that she was a model.

"I am a model. I don't belong here."

You could tell that she had great manners. Each of the girls had a yellow or brown plastic drinking cup. They put their names on it to know which cup was theirs because they all look the same. I could see how she held her cup when she was having tea. Very classic, putting the two fingers together, and the little finger up. I could tell that this girl had some class.

I lead the class, but I try to have the girls do most of the talking. I want to know what's on their minds, what's happening to them. I don't ask why they're in prison, because that's not part of my function. If they want to share, that's different. Most of the time I just want to know how they feel today. A lot of times they'll share something. They'll open their heart and come out with something about their families, or where they come from.

This girl seemed like she came from a really good family. And she was having a very hard time being in prison. She cried and kept repeating, "I don't belong here, I don't belong here."

The other inmates reached out to her, tried to calm her down. They told her, "It's going to be fine. It's going to be okay." I didn't see her again and I'll never know what happened to her after that.

Scheila

This morning, I am in line, and Tanya is about three people ahead of me. Carmen is already sitting at a table. There's nobody sitting at the table near her or around her. The tables are round, and there are six round stools at each one. They're all cemented to the ground.

I am surveying the room.

Okay, I'm going to sit there when I'm ready.

I see Tanya grab her food. She hits Carmen's shoulder with her tray as she walks by. Hard. The force almost pushes her back off the stool.

I already have my tray of food, and I'm watching the whole thing. As Tanya is looking over her shoulder at Carmen, smiling, walking past her.

Something in me… something in me, I don't know
what…

What it is, is that I saw myself in Carmen. In my
story, I'm not thinking about a specific person like
Tanya. For me, it was the realities of *life* that were
my torment. The way Tanya was constantly bullying
Carmen and making her feel like she was less than
nothing. That's the same way *life* had treated me.
Life was always trying to knock me down. Most of
my *life* had always served me such a bad time.

I refused to stand by and watch it any longer. It
was my moment and, finally, I had a chance to stand
up to the world that was always pushing me down.
I didn't see Tanya anymore. In this moment, I was
fighting *life*.

It's almost as if my feet have grown wings. I fly
on top of her, and I commence to beating her with
my tray. And beating her. And beating her. And I
don't stop. Everyone's screaming. Everyone's
yelling. And everyone's in a circle around us.

My cellie is making sure that nobody jumps in. I
have my family. Like I told you before, women
develop families in prison. And my family is ready
to fight anyone who is going to jump in. But there
is nobody jumping in. It's me on top of this woman,
pummeling her, and I don't stop.

Then I feel this mass of hurt. It's as if something is ripping my side open when it hits me. When I wake up there are two COs standing over me.

They come and they body slam me, and at the same time, a spray of mace hits my face. I can't breathe and I'm coughing. They're handcuffing me. And I'm blind. I hear all the screams; I hear all the noise. I can't smell anything else, but I smell pepper and it's in my throat and I'm gagging.

I feel my body being lifted off the ground and I then don't feel anything solid anymore. It's like I'm floating, and I am floating. My hands are tied to my back and there are shackles on my feet. The shackles are tied to another chain that's tied to my hands. I'm almost hogtied, and I'm overwhelmed with pain.

I hear the COs talking. "What happened?"

"Do you know what happened?"

"I don't know. This is crazy!"

I can hear them, but I can't make out much of what they're saying because I have a ringing in my ear. I don't know if it was from the impact of hitting the floor. It must have been about three COs that tackled me. They must have felt like they had to get me off of this woman quickly to eliminate the threat.

I don't know. I think about it... Could I have killed her? Maybe. If I kept going, and going, and going. But I don't think I would have taken it there.

But then again, I remember losing control and not caring anymore. It felt good, I say to myself, as they carry me away.

I hear a door open, and there's a mass of clanging metal doors.

And I feel cold.

But this wasn't a day I'd rate as low as a "1."
This was only a "2."

Sioni

There are a lot of girls that have ink on their bodies. Sometimes it's something that means a lot to them like the names of their kids. Or it might be something about how they feel about their boyfriends or themselves. There was one girl who had a very large tattoo. She said, "This is my ex. I got a tattoo when I went out with him and now, he's gone, and I'm stuck with it!"

Nora was a light-skinned woman, with green eyes, gray hair. She had a lot of tattoos on her arms. She came to my class and I remember she always sat on the left side of the table. One time I looked at Nora and I asked her, "What do those tattoos mean?"

"These tattoos tell my life story."

I was impressed. "They're beautiful!"

And most of them really were very beautiful. She had this big rose on her arm, and I asked her what the rose meant. She began to tell me that this is how her mother used to see her when she was a young girl, like a rose.

I also noticed that she had some dark things on her other arm. I asked her, "What does that mean?"

She said, "These are some things that I've gone through in my life."

She was very sweet, and I began to like her a lot.

One Sunday, as I was walking out of the unit, I saw Nora. I'll never forget her because I could see her bright green eyes. I said, "Okay, girls, I'll see you next week!" And that's when she said, "You know, I won't be here. I'm leaving this week."

"Oh, I'm so happy for you! You're leaving! I'm definitely looking forward to seeing what God has for you in your life! To see what it is that He's going to do!"

The following week, I went back to the unit, but I could tell right away that something bad had happened. It was easy to see that all the women were very sad.

"What happened? What's going on, girls? Why are you acting this way? Why are you so down?"

They told me that they had found Nora in a hotel. It was all over the news. She had taken some pills as she had in the past. Because she had been clean for a while and she wasn't used to the drugs anymore, she overdosed, and she died from it. It was pretty devastating to all of us.

I can never forget her face. Sometimes I close my eyes and I see her, even after all this time. Here's the thing. She was telling me, "I'm not going to see you." And I didn't see her ever again.

I've seen a lot of people in prison that come and go, and I never see them again because they overdose when they leave. I loved Nora. She was special to me, as all the women are, and I thought she was going to be okay the last time I saw her.

I remember looking back at her and waving my two fingers, and saying, "Bye!" She looked at me and gave me a thumbs up like she was saying, "I'm going to be okay." She looked at me, and then she looked down quickly. And then I didn't see her again. She was in the hotel room, overdosed, on the bed. She was 33 years old.

" 2 "

CAUGHT OFF GUARD

Scheila

Everything is cold. All of a sudden, I feel the floor. They throw me into a cell. The floor feels almost wet, but it isn't. It's like a cement floor that is frozen. They take the restraints off me. They tell me if I move, they'll shoot me with a pellet gun to disable me.

I'm not going to move, Guy. I know what happened and I know where I am.

Everyone knows that if you break the rules or you fight, you're going into solitary confinement. This means every day has 23 hours of lockdown. After they remove the handcuffs, I lie there. No one treats me for the pepper spray, so I have all this stuff in my eyes and in my mouth.

I'm feeling around and I'm crawling, and I find the toilet. I'm so desperate to get this pepper spray out of my eyes that I take the toilet bowl water, and I start splashing it on my face.

I start crying. I start sobbing. My body starts shaking uncontrollably. My adrenaline is rushing, and I start shaking uncontrollably. I am in shock. It almost feels like when you stand up after being in a car crash—that disorientated and numb feeling.

I look down. After a few minutes pass, I start to open my eyes a little. Everything is starting to form shapes. I look around and I see it's a tiny room.

I can stretch my arms out, and my arms touch each side of the wall. It takes five steps from front to back, and three steps from one side to the other. I'm looking and there's a metal sheet to sleep on—there's no mattress—and a toilet and a sink. That's it. There's no window. There's a giant door with a slot in it.

I look around me. I sit on the metal slab and I look at my clothes. My county khakis are covered in blood. I automatically get scared.

Did she cut me? Where did she cut me?

I start stripping down naked to look for any cuts or stabs.

Sometimes you won't feel a shank. I've heard many women say that to me. After you've been stabbed and someone puts a hole in you, sometimes you don't feel it. Sometimes you don't feel getting cut.

I'm looking and there're no cuts on me. There's an aluminum sheet that's hanging on the wall that's supposed to be a mirror. People who were here before me had written all kinds of graffiti on it; carved all kinds of things. But there's one corner that's a little shiny, so I look to see if I have any marks on my face. Any abrasions. I have a couple of scratches on my neck from when she put her arms up to try to choke me, to make me stop.

I'm sad. I'm cold. I'm scared. And I'm sitting there all alone. Someone comes over a speaker in the cell.

"Inmate Jimenez. The inmate that you've assaulted does not want to press charges on you. Would you like to press charges on the inmate?"

"Of course not."

"Okay. No problem." The microphone cuts out.

I start to hear people screaming. People kicking the door. I start to hear people cursing, singing, all kinds of things. I go to my slot and I listen.

I can hear people saying, "Who are you?"

"What are you down here for?"

And it begins to sink in. I'm in the hole.

No one came to me that night. No one came to check on me. No CO came back. There was nothing like that. No nurse came to follow through. I just laid there.

I had put my clothes back on after I figured out what had happened. I was taking it all in mentally. The clothes were bloody, but when you go to the hole, your stuff doesn't come with you. A change of clothes didn't come until they sent all my things down, which was the following morning.

When you first arrive in jail, you are given khaki pants and a khaki shirt. But there's a t-shirt you wear underneath it. So, I was able to remove my khaki shirt, and I still had on my white thermal. I remember putting my white thermal on and leaving my panties on and lying there on this metal slab.

I remember lying there, looking at the ceiling.

If I died, this is probably what it would feel like.

The metal slab reminded me of a morgue.

Am I fighting the inevitable? Is this what's supposed to happen to me? Am I supposed to die here? I already feel dead. I think maybe death would be the best outcome.

⌘

Thoughts of suicide crept in so fast.

I don't know if it was because of the lack of space, or if it was the hopelessness I had—as if I had lost everything. But the minute I arrived, I realized that

I would be locked in this cell for 23 hours a day. Mentally, there's no way to prepare you for that. You just know that's what it is.

I had thought about suicide before I went to the hole, but it wasn't as real as this. I had thought of suicide in a way of wondering if I did it, what would happen. Who would be favored by my death? But when I was in the hole, it was different. I was thinking about the actual ways I could do it.

I remember one by one, pulling the strings out of the blanket they gave me. I didn't go too far in between strings because I was afraid the CO would notice. After a while, I had a ball of string. I thought if I layered the strings thick enough, I could maybe make a noose. The thought of suicide now became a reality. It was more than a fleeting thought. It was a *want* to put into action. The idea of suicide stuck with me.

It's that way for a lot of people. I know it's going to sound perverse, but it's also a form of entertainment. We were locked up for 23 out of 24 hours. We could only read so many books. We could only stare at the wall for so long. We could only do so many things in our tiny, tiny box. So, we started to find other ways to entertain ourselves. Even if that was to entertain the thought of suicide.

⌘

The next day, the CO came and brought the things from my cell to me down in the hole. Then they handcuffed me and took me in front of a prison board, and the board let me know what I was in there for. They told me that I was to remain in the hole until my trial date.

I didn't know how long that would be. You don't know when you're going to get your trial date until it's time for you to go to trial unless you plead guilty.

So, for the remainder of my time here, I'm going to be in the hole.

Because it was my first time in the hole, they told me that they would look at sending me back if I was on good behavior.

Whatever.

That was one of my worst days of being incarcerated.

I ended up staying almost two months in the hole. Then they released me back to general population because of over-crowding. By then, the inmate that I had "assaulted" had already left.

I wonder if I'd had a split second more to think before I went animalistic on her, if there is anything I would have done differently. What could I have done to keep this from happening?

I believe I should have talked to her. Would the outcome still have been the same? Yeah, possibly. Even most likely. But I could have talked to her and

I could have asked her why she was picking on my friend.

Knowing how fighting works, she probably would have had the upper hand. She would have caught me off guard by taking the first hit. So, in a way, I should have talked to her. But in a way, I don't think there was another alternative that would have worked. I'm not condoning fighting, because in a prison fight there are no winners. But sometimes fighting is the only way when you're locked up. Sometimes it's the only way to get a point across. Sometimes it's the only way to mend a relationship. It's the weirdest thing.

I had been in plenty of fights prior to being incarcerated. But I had never gotten in a fight with a grown woman. It's different from being in a schoolgirl fight, or even getting in a fistfight with your brother. I'd recently turned 18, and I was fighting an adult woman who was a veteran in the system, and a biker woman at that. There's a whole different feeling.

When you're fighting out on the street, you already assume that you're going to beat that person up. When you're incarcerated, there's so much that goes into it. You don't know if you're going to get jumped. You don't know if you're going to get stabbed. You don't know if that person knows someone in the next pod over. Whether when you come out of the hole—when you go into that next pod—this person is there, waiting to get revenge. To beat you up. To stab you. To cut you. To jump you. It's so much deeper than just a fistfight. There're all kinds of politics that go into it.

⌘

I thought that the first fight would be my lowest point. But later there would be a time that shook me all the way to my core. It was the day I was caught with my guard down. That would be the day *I* got beat up.

Before I got sent back to the hole the second time, I had pretty much been running that pod. I had been what they call a pod boss. A pod boss does as they wish, and nobody says anything to them. For the most part, the pod boss doesn't bother anybody. They just want to do their own thing. They don't want to be told what to do by anybody.

I didn't set out to be a pod boss. It just happened. When I was sent back to the general population, I wasn't returned to my original cell. Instead, I was sent to the next pod over.

Everything is made with glass, so you could see the pod right across from you, like looking through a window at your neighbor's yard. Everyone can see everything. Everyone saw what happened in that fight. They were in their dayroom; we were in our dayroom. So, everyone knew who I was.

People look out for you when you're incarcerated and word travels very fast in jail. People know you're coming up from the hole before you do. When I came up from the hole, it was during lockdown, so only the trustees were out cleaning the day room. I went to my cell and met my new cellie, and already the trustees started slipping kites under my door.

Kites are notes. The kind of notes you slip to officers or the notes you send to other inmates. They might say, "Welcome to 'A' Pod," or "I got you," or "Coffee on me after lockdown." I had coffee slipped to me in a bag, I had sugar slipped to me, I had extra Kool-Aid packets. It was like a welcoming committee. Like a welcome mat. And something triggered in my brain. So that's how it works. The more violent you are, the more you're rewarded.

That's wrong because that's not how it is. But that's how it felt. I felt like a queen. I felt like I was on top of the world. I had inmates I didn't even know giving me things—just because! They had witnessed me go animalistic on another person. In a way, it's as if they wanted me to accept them. Wanted me to notice them. I don't know if it's because they didn't want problems, but I found out later on, that's never how it works in prison.

Everybody wants somebody—to get something out of them. There are no friendships in prison. There's no real sisterhood in prison. Everybody has something they can bring to the table. And if fearlessness is what you can bring to the table, people are going to want you around them. They know when push comes to shove, if it's got to get crazy, you're going to throw down. You're going to be fast to fight. You're not going to care. You're an inmate who doesn't care. I remember that. I remember the whole thing like a welcoming party. I had people screaming my name who I had not even met.

From then on, my approach was very different. I became very, very mean to people. The person who I was when I was in the pod before—defending someone—is what got me in trouble. And then when I moved to the pod across, I became the bully. I became that person who was now feasting on the weak. It does something to you. I don't know if it was the hole. I don't know if it was my time in the dark, but I almost became like a predator. And everybody looked like prey.

⌘

There was an inmate by the name of Irene. Irene was a very tall, African American woman in her 40s, and she was addicted to crack cocaine. She once told me that she had six children, and they were all in the system or with relatives.

Irene had a girlfriend who was in the pod with me, and her girlfriend and I had become very good friends. Almost to the point where we would share snacks and things. And Irene didn't like that, even though I, myself, was not in a homosexual relationship. There was absolutely nothing at all—it was a platonic, straight friendship on my part.

I learned a lesson about being in jail the hard way. If you befriend a gay person, everyone assumes that you two are together. That you are doing something together. A large population of the women who are incarcerated end up with other women because they're lonely. That's just how it works. And that's why Irene thought that I was a Casanova.

On that day, I was on the phone with my mother. As soon as I hung up, I turned around, and she was right there. Before I even had a chance to ask her what was wrong, the look on her face told me what I needed to know. I remember feeling her hand grab me by the hair, and she pushed my head back against the phone. And it felt as though my skull had burst open.

I fell right to the ground. She came behind me and she started choking me and I couldn't do anything about it. I was kicking, and I tried to grab her hair but was too short. When you do so many drugs, it destroys your hair and your nails, and the crack cocaine she did had thinned out all her hair. I remember trying to grab her hair, but there was no hair there to grab. Luckily, Irene's girlfriend got her off me. But of course, the COs were already headed to the door. The COs used their good old pepper spray, everybody dropped down, and they dragged me off to the hole again.

I was caught off guard. It made me question how on-point I was, more than anything, because she caught me off guard. I think about it all the time.

It's a cycle. When I got back from the hole after my fight with the biker woman, I felt invincible. So, my second fight was destined to not be victorious. My second fight ended in me being choked out.

It's a cycle and there's always somebody who's tougher than you. There's always somebody bigger than you. There's always somebody stronger than you. So as tough as you want to pretend you are, there's going to be somebody who can look past that. Somebody who's been through worse. Somebody who's gotten in even more scuffles. Somebody who's gotten in even more fights. That's just how it is.

⌘

I think about it more often now that I'm a Christian. How often does the devil catch me off guard? How often do I let my guard down? How often do I forget to pray? How often do I forget to read my Bible?

When I forget these things, I'm letting my guard down. The devil can creep in at any moment. I wouldn't have blamed it on "the devil" back then. I would have said I had to fight because of the code. But I recognize now that I'm not spiritually strong if I'm not aware of what the devil can do to me.

This was my very lowest point. I had lost plenty of fights before then. No one wins every fight. Losing a fight was nothing. But because I was caught off guard, I would say that this day is definitely my lowest day.

" 3 "

LOSING EVERYTHING

Sioni

There was a young girl, maybe in her twenties, who was new to the unit. She was very broken. I was sharing a sermon about the choices we have to make, and she cried all through the discussion. I couldn't tell exactly what had happened to make her react this way.

She mentioned that when she has troubles; she uses drugs. That's what she has done for the last couple of years. She's coping with her pain through drugs.

Some choose to use the prison as a revolving door. I spoke to a girl last week. She said that she *didn't start using drugs until she was 27. But now she's in her mid-forties and she's still in prison because of drugs. She says this time is going to be the last time that she's in prison.*

She had been using prison as an escape. Each time she ran out of money or places to live, she would commit a crime. That way she could go back to jail and have a place to stay and have a hot meal. In fact, some of the girls tell me that's what they do if they don't have a home to go to. They just get in trouble and go back to prison. Why? Because the prison gives them temporary shelter.

Scheila

I was angry.

Angry at a God I didn't know. Angry at a God I always blamed. Angry at a God I demanded change from, even though I never changed myself.

I was angry at the world. I was angry at my mother. I was angry at my childhood. I was angry at my upbringing. I was angry at my choices. I was angry to be alive. I was angry that I could breathe.

It was like a jungle in there. It's like everyone in there is ranked an animal, and your rage and your anger are what defines your ranking. When you show this prison anger and bitterness, it's like a porcupine letting off its needles. That's what you have to do. You have to put off this presentation of hardness. Of solid rock. That's where I was at. I was angry to the point where it almost felt normal to be so angry.

I was sad. Hopeless. Broken down. Beaten.

I was an emotional mess. I was stressed out. Stressed beyond anything I'd felt in the past. I was so stressed out while I was incarcerated that I was losing hair by the chunks.

I missed life on the outside. And at the same time, I was angry at how life was for me on the outside. I was sad about my situation. Sad that I couldn't do anything about my situation. Sad that I couldn't get water out of the fridge when I wanted to or go to the bathroom without someone watching.

And at the same time, I was happy. I know that sounds crazy, but I was happy, too. I was finally somewhere where I knew that nothing could hurt me without being able to defend myself. That the world couldn't hurt me as much because I was away from the world.

The world in prison felt safer in the way that the elements of your day-to-day abuse cannot affect you in prison. You take on a different form of abuse, but you're no longer a victim in your own world. It's a different type of victimization. You become a victim of the system. You become a victim of rules. You become a victim of conformity because now you are going to be told what to do. You no longer have a choice. You no longer have the freedom to do what you want. So, you become a victim in that aspect.

I learned from serving time with a lot of women who committed murder. Most of the time it was in retaliation for some form of abuse. They may have been victims of alcohol or drugs. They may be victims of physical abuse from their spouse or partner. They might be in an abusive relationship where they're forced to sell their bodies. Whatever the reason, they are no longer victims of that scenario anymore. They've taken whatever steps they had to. And now they find themselves in the place they are now, which is incarcerated.

They are incarcerated, but at least they don't have to worry about their pimps beating on them. They don't have to worry about a john stabbing them or raping them and not paying for their services. They think, "Yeah, I'm here, I don't have my freedom, but was my freedom really freedom?"

I've seen it, unfortunately, for a lot of mentally ill. It's because they don't have the right type of support or the right type of anything. When they get outside, they have to wander mentally. At least when they're incarcerated, they get medication every day, for whatever it is. They get it from the doctors. And they get certain needs met that haven't been met on the street. A lot of these women don't have jobs. The ones that do have jobs, after they're incarcerated, they're not going back to their jobs. Employers aren't going to take back someone who's been incarcerated, whatever the reason for the crime.

A lot of these women lose their children in the process. So, they go back to no husband, and no children—their children are now in the foster care system. You think of all the chaos that they deal with. At least in prison, you deal with a certain set of rules, but you know those rules apply to all others around you. Not like on the streets where there's no code of ethics. No one is spared. It doesn't matter. The streets have a way of forcing you to live a certain way, whereas prison forces you to adapt to a certain way of life.

There is a large portion of women in the prison population who have a mental illness. From a big scale to a tiny scale, you see it in a lot of inmates. I also believe that it's because of the abuse they've absorbed their whole lives, as children, as teenagers, as adults. That abuse does something to the mind, and it's never the same again.

People might be surprised that people go back to jail for safety. Many assume that ex-cons go back because they didn't learn from their mistakes.

I think people do learn lessons. Just not the ones we thought they should learn.

Sioni

I was talking to an inmate last week, and she was surprised that there were so many young people in prison. She said, "When I first went to prison, I was 20 years old. These days the girls are so young, and they've already started using drugs. Unfortunately, they get caught in the system and end up in prison. Sadly, they get out and go back to the only environment that they know, and the cycle begins again.

Before they go to prison, they start with the confidence of youth, thinking that they will do better than the generations before them. That is, until they're incarcerated. It can be a real shock once the reality hits.

Once they're in prison, they often look up to the more mature inmates. These older ladies become like their mom. Making connections is definitely a big thing in prison, whether it's a good connection or a bad connection. Unfortunately, you have the ones who make bad choices. They start changing the way they see things and even the way they act.

I can give you an example. I had a girl who had been coming to the Bible study, and she had been doing well. Last week, when I was there on Sunday, and I could tell she didn't want to be there. That was not normal for her. I pretended not to notice *how she acted. I went on, as usual, asking each of them, "Are you okay?"*

Not everybody feels the same way every day. But I noticed that she didn't seem to be getting anything from the class. She didn't act the same as she usually did. When the class finished, and she walked away, I asked the other girls, "What happened to her? Is she not feeling well today?"

They said, "Yeah, she was being ugly. She started hanging around with a different woman, and that's why she's acting this way now."

This girl had been in the group for five or six months. But then she changed. She didn't talk to me much. She was upset and very bitter at the system. And now she had negative things to say, like complaining about how the prisons dealt with the inmates. It seemed that she had lost focus on the positive teachings of Christ.

I noticed something about her when I was talking about being connected and staying connected. I started talking about how we need to choose to forgive people who have hurt us. I noticed that she turned her face to look out the window. Her eyes got a little watery like she was about ready to cry. By the way she was acting, she might have been dealing with something that was difficult for her. She was keeping herself separate—disconnecting— from the group. I don't know the exact reason, but certainly, she was reacting to what I said about people that we love the most. How sometimes they hurt us. Even our own family.

In a situation like this, I believe that there's a reason why somebody who might not want to be in the class, comes anyway. It could be that the Holy Spirit draws them to that place.

All I can do is to let them go through what they're going to go through and pray for them. And sometimes I stop, and I ask them, "Are you okay? Do you want to share how you feel? You don't have to. But if you feel like you want to share something, you're welcome to share." Sometimes they say, "no." But sometimes they say, "yes!"

Scheila

There was such a cocktail of emotions when I was in prison. There were feelings that didn't make sense. But what I felt the most when I was incarcerated was *alone.*

Alone. Loneliness like I'd never felt before.

Abandonment. Everyone had abandoned me. The judge had abandoned me. The lawyers. The world had abandoned me. Everyone who looked at me, looked like they'd already given up on me. I thought even God had given up on me.

Out of all the feelings, even more than my anger, I felt loneliness. All the time. Even if I was in a room full of 50 other women that felt as lonely as I did.

We felt alone. Everybody was alone. Nobody had anybody. When you're incarcerated, you're by yourself. You have to fend for yourself. So that's how I felt, mostly.

Just alone.

Sioni

There are those with a family that supports them by putting money on their "books." This is money they can use to buy things at the commissary. Sometimes they share with the ones that don't have money to use for themselves.

Some have families that withdrew their support before they ever got to prison. I've had ladies who've told me that they've had to live in a tent because their parents told them, "I don't want you in here. If you want to, you can put a tent up, but keep outside the house."

One time I was talking about a story of a woman in the Bible who was an outsider. One of the women shared with me, "I feel like I'm an outsider." She told me how her family threw her out and she had to sleep in a tent outside, even in the winter.

So, she was literally an "outsider." That was pretty devastating.

Scheila

They said there was a chance that I could be let out of the hole for good behavior. But I was labeled a dangerous inmate. The thing is, there was a certain no-fear factor that the COs picked up on. I guess they know when an inmate has no fear. When they've lost everything—their minds and their material world. There's no longer a conscience. They're already being punished for whatever it is, so there's no fear of further punishment. In a way, it's like prisoners think, *What are you gonna do? Are you going to kill me? You might be doing me a favor.* That mentality is what worries COs more than anything—the inmates who have nothing to lose. Those inmates don't care.

I think for some reason they sensed that in me. And in a way, I look back and I realize that I was that inmate. I didn't care. I felt like I had nothing to lose. Even though I had a mother who supported me and loved me and wrote to me every day, I felt like it was too little, too late.

I could have looked for a way to fix my relationship with my mother. I could have tried to fix my whole mindset and grow from the experience. Instead, I grew angrier because of my experience. I grew more desperate for attention. I grew more desperate for any means of love. And I walked around in a constant state of anger.

So many women who are incarcerated feel as though they lost everything. They lost their children. They lost their marriage. They lost whatever status in the society that they once had. Whatever job. Whatever school. They feel like they lost it all.

That's when you go into this despair of losing yourself.

4

EVERY TUESDAY

Sioni

We pour so much encouragement into these girls who are in prison. Then we find out one of those girls that we've been pouring so much into has overdosed and died. The first reaction might be to second guess our purpose and to wonder if we're doing things right. But this confusion doesn't come from God.

Sometimes there are the ones where all in a moment it seems like they really hear you. Sometimes it feels like they get it. They understand, they're ready to go! They have the tools for living on the outside that we've taught them. Life skills that are waiting and ready to go when they're released.

They seem ready. Then you see them again, and it seems like all they accomplished went down the drain. Either they got a phone call, or somebody gave them the wrong news. It can be an emotional roller coaster.

Some of the girls don't want anything to do with God. For whatever reason, they feel like God has abandoned them. That He has forgotten about them. My goal is to encourage them and to lift their spirits up. I tell them that being in prison is not God's will for their lives. There are choices we make, and this is the result of the choices we've made. God has nothing to do with that. I do lift them up and pray that they realize that being in prison doesn't define who they are. They are who God created them to be, and they are loved!

Sometimes we all gather around the table in the room where we have the study, and we pray for the ones that cannot come out. Those are the girls who are in the maximum security unit—the hole. They are completely isolated. The girls in this unit are always very down and depressed.

When I go to that section of the prison, I have to sit inside this huge bubble-glass thing in the unit. The girls there have been locked down and they can't come out of their cells. The only window to the outside that they have is the slot in the door that their meals are passed through.

Some have a lot of mental issues, and you can hear them screaming, cursing, crying, laughing... all kinds of outbursts. I might try to give them a class, but it's very hard for them to hear because of the screaming.

I'm not supposed to, but I have gotten close enough to grab their hands through that little hole and pray for them. They seem to really need that physical touch, A lot of times they show me pictures of their family. They say, "pray for me." It's heartbreaking, but that's exactly what I do.

When I leave that unit, I tell them that it doesn't matter how things look, I know that God is working! He's working behind the scenes. We might not see it. But we can trust that He's working.

I believe in His Word. And I know that when I say what I say, they might not get it at that time. But I know that one day they'll be using what I've taught them.

Scheila

I got a taste of hope for the first time in a long time. It came completely out of the blue—so unexpected, but so needed.

I was working on a scheme, trying to figure a way to make money while I was incarcerated. Usually, I had people come to me to get their hair done. I was in my cell talking with my bunkmate. I remember the CO knocking from the other side of the door.

"Inmate Jimenez, you have a visitor."

I didn't get visitors because all my family was on the east coast. I was by myself at 18, in a Washington State Department of Corrections women's prison. I was the youngest person in my pod, and one of the three youngest inmates in the building.

Beyond that, it wasn't even a visitation day.

My cellmate said, "Oh, it's probably your lawyer." That made sense. They would come to see us when they got out of court. Lawyers were allowed to pull us out of the pod whenever they needed to see us.

I glanced back at my cellie and turned around to follow the officer. As we left the pod, he stopped to put handcuffs on me.

He took me down a long, white hallway. The floor was a glossy, gray linoleum like a hospital floor. We came to the one door in the hallway. This is where you have your meetings with your lawyer, but we passed right by. Now I had no idea who would be visiting me.

We made a right and boarded the elevator that was there. The CO told me to face the wall. "Don't look at me," he barked. I turned to face the wall, and the elevator started down. The door opened to reveal another long hallway. This one had a lot more doors. Now we were going to another part of the jail that I'd never been to before. The hallway led into another that ended at the visitation room.

The room could hold about 50 visitors, but there was only one man in the room, obviously waiting to talk to me. Later I would find out that he was able to come on this odd day because he was a spiritual advisor. Apparently, he was *my* spiritual advisor. And he wasn't seeing anyone else. He was there specifically to see me.

The room was filled with little visitation booths. The booths were divided by wooden walls and there was glass between you and your visitor. I couldn't see who the person was at first, but I could see that the phone was waiting. It was lying on the table, ready to be picked up, as if the conversation was ready to begin.

I saw a man there. He was a Hispanic man, balding, a heavy-set guy. I noticed right away that he was almost glowing. He had this glow, and he was smiling from ear-to-ear. The first thing I remember seeing about this man, besides his giant smile, was his big gold chain. It had a little island of Puerto Rico emblem hanging from it.

I approached and picked up the phone. I was very angry.

"Who are you and what do you want? Why are you wasting my time?"

He said to me, "Scheila, it's nice to meet you. Your mother, Sioni, reached out to me and she wants me to start coming to visit you.

"I'm a pastor at a local church. We got an email from your mother. I wanted to come and visit you. Is it okay if I come and visit you and read you a little from the Bible? Can I come and visit you from time to time?"

At first, everything in me wanted to start sobbing. At the same time, I didn't know how to feel. I was still so numb. Still living, but not really living. I was alive. I had a heartbeat. But I wasn't *really alive.*

So, what this man said registered to me as, *Oh, my mom—the Jesus freak—meets another Jesus freak. Now he's going to come and tell me how wrong I am and all the horrible things I've done. He's going to tell me how I deserve to be here.*

But I told him, "Sure. You can come to visit me." We sat down to have our first conversation.

The first thing he said was, "I remember coming here to visit my son."

And the wall I had put up tumbled to the ground. I *saw* this man now for who he really was. His eyes no longer seemed like eyes that were judging me. He was someone who my mom was. I knew that what he told me was real. I knew this man *understood*. He didn't see the problem. He saw *me*.

I sat there, and I spoke with this pastor. We had a great conversation that first time.

Pastor Jorge faithfully visited me. Every week. Every Tuesday.

Every Tuesday.

Sioni

In the New Testament book of John, in Chapter 15, Jesus is teaching the disciples using a parable to illustrate His point. He tells them that He is the Vine, and we are the branches.

> **"...If you remain in me and I in you, you will bear much fruit..."** *John 15:5* (NIV)

Being connected to the vine is like our relationship with Christ. This is such a perfect example of God's connection.

Think about how the vines grow. They tangle up with each other in the same way that we need each other. That's how God created us to be—to have each other.

I explain this to the women. I try to cheer them up, and I tell them that if they stay connected to

Jesus, they will not be empty. The ultimate is knowing that God is the source of our life. Stay connected to the Vine and you will produce good results.

Of course, if you disconnect, or stay to yourself and avoid other people, you'll start to get results that are not from God. Nothing can be fruitful if it's not fed by the Vine. Without the nourishment that comes from the source (God), the branch (believers) will just dry up and die. It is such a simple verse, yet it's so powerful.

Of course, hearing this message is easy. Living the message is very difficult, but not impossible.

Sometimes the women disconnect from the branch. They may not ever want to leave their unit. They become like fruits that lose their color. They start drying up and they fade away. It can be because either they've gotten a call—or they haven't gotten a call. Or something like not having any money on the books for the commissary. These things will cause them to disconnect but cannot fill the emptiness. If it did, it would only be temporary.

Others are so connected to God that it doesn't matter. They say, "You know what? This is just a temporary period. I know things are going to get better."

In this world, it is not easy to abide in Christ. Why? Because of the world and our sinful desires. He knows our power comes from being connected to our Maker. Because of this, he will do everything possible to keep us disconnected from our connection with the Lord. How does he do that? One of the weapons he uses is discouragement to draw people away either from churches or even God.

I know a lot of people who say they don't want anything to do with God. They say, "While I'm in prison, I'm not with my family. I'm not with my kids. I'm not at their graduation. I'm not with my son or my daughter whose birthday it is." The list goes on. So much of what goes on with their family is missed.

All these things Satan uses to discourage people. He steals their time. He steals their faith. Their hope. Their confidence. Their peace. It's very hard to stay connected to Christ when you are in prison. Very hard.

To abide in Christ is to choose a relationship with Him. And when we do, we find that Christ has already chosen to have a relationship with us. And He sends the Holy Spirit to live in us.

How do you abide in Christ? How do you get and stay connected? One way is to read the Bible, always making time to read the Word of God. Because we need to set the Word of God into our hearts. Simple, right? But hard to do sometimes. When you change the way you think, it will change the things you do.

You will learn God's truth from the Bible. His words can be trusted. Some people who come to prison bring their own understanding of the truth. But the only real truth is God's truth. And that's the truth that will set you free.

Another way to stay connected to Christ is through prayer. Many people say they don't know how to pray. I tell them to just speak to Him. It's that simple. He doesn't need to hear fancy or memorized words. Be yourself and talk to Him in your own authentic voice. He already knows what's in your heart. God wants a relationship with you.

When we live together, connected to Christ, we produce good results. You need to ask yourself, what kinds of results are you producing in your life now? The Bible tells us what God promises us.

"But the fruit of the Spirit is love, joy, peace, forbearance, kindness, goodness, faithfulness, gentleness and self-control. Against such things there is no law." *Galatians 5:22-23* (NIV)

And what gives bad results? Emotions and the things that we do because of them. Change comes by renewing your thoughts with God's word.

We have to learn how to deal with our emotions. When our emotions control us, we say things and we do things that will get us into huge trouble. Some people end up incarcerated because of what they've done or said because of their emotions. We need to understand that we can control our emotions. Our emotions should not control us.

What happens when we give in to our emotions? We fight with jealousy, fear, vanity, and more. We're fighting with so many distractions. In reality, the only thing worth fighting for is to stay in a relationship with Christ. Talk to Him.

I'll usually ask the class to give an example of a time when they stayed connected with Christ. I'll also ask them to describe a time when they felt disconnected.

One girl said she was connected before she came to prison. She was going to church with her mom and was trying to do the right things. Trying to do the right things was what made her feel connected.

"But," she continued, "I started to hang around with older friends. Before long I started going to places where I shouldn't have gone. I got into trouble and ended up in jail." She said, "When I came to prison I was totally disconnected because of my bad choices."

She found that she was spiritually dried up. It got to the point where she didn't want to have anything to do with God. And then her emotions started to take over.

"I thought that God was not there for me. That I was going to church and doing these things but now

He was not there for me." This thinking contributed to why she got disconnected.

But now she was reconnecting. Talking about it had her tearing up because the class understood and cared about her. God used me to minister to the class. They ministered to each other. Connections were being made.

Some people will stay connected and some people will disconnect instead. What it comes down to is that it's about choices. You can't force people to want to know about God. And certainly, you can't demand that someone have a relationship with God. It's their choice. It's their choice to do right. To want to be better. To get out of prison and to become the person God created them to be."

Scheila

I pushed the chair back. I turned and walked back down the long hallway, up the elevator, and down the other hallway, back to my cell. This time it wasn't my surroundings that I noticed. It was what was happening inside.

I felt a warmth in my heart. My heart was beating. I remember my feet being numb. These are the little things I remember! My feet were numb, but I felt a warmth in my chest. I felt good. I felt appreciated. I felt like somebody cared. I knew my mother cared. But I was always fighting the idea because somehow, I blamed her that I ended up being incarcerated. Now that I'm an adult and I look back... I was happy. I found hope!

But at the same time, I had so many questions. I felt sad that I couldn't leave with him. I felt sad that I couldn't go to his church that he told me about. I kept wondering what his church was like. I wondered what his wife was like. I wondered about his son because he told me his son was no longer incarcerated; he was in ministry. I started thinking about hope. I started feeling hopeful.

I just got a visitor!

It felt good! I felt happy.

Will he come back?

He asked me if he could, and I told him, "Absolutely. Please come back."

But I didn't really expect him to. I had lost all hope in people and in what they would say. So, if anybody promised me anything, I automatically checked it off in my mind. *Well, they're going to do the opposite.* That's just the way my mind worked. I couldn't trust anyone.

When he said, "I'll be back next week then," I thought, *Oh, no, you won't. You won't be back.* This would be like every other person in the world that dealt with me. They were in it to get what they could for themselves. *I'll forever be that person you*

come and take from. And that will be it. You'll
move on to the next thing, next week. And you'll
forget all about me.

But that's not what happened. It's not what happened at all.

My hopefulness after meeting Pastor Jorge didn't last long, though. The atmosphere in prison... Everyone was so angry. It's almost as if you can cut through the air with a knife because of the tension that's in there. I got as far as going into the pod. When you walk in and you hear people screaming, you hear people fighting, people arguing. All the noise. All the chaos. The smells. The dirtiness. The filth. It took all of five minutes when I got back to where the jungle was. My newfound hopefulness lasted until I laid back on my bunk in my cell.

⌘

Pastor Jorge told me that my mom had been in contact with his secretary. He said that they had developed a very good relationship. They were talking to each other quite often. I thought that was interesting. My mom's always forming relationships with people.

She doesn't even know this lady. How does she talk to her?

He said that he had spoken to my mother and that she seemed like a wonderful person. On that very first day, he made a point to let me know that my mother loved me. He must have told me that three times. And he told me that Jesus loved me. And that God had not given up on me. And that He still had a purpose for my life.

Then he had questions for me. He wanted to know how I was, whether I was eating, whether anyone was hurting me. The way he spoke showed me that he was really concerned. He wanted to know how the officers were treating me. He just wanted to know how I was doing.

I guess he wanted to know for my mother's sake because my mother was telling him how concerned she was. She wanted reassurance that I was okay.

My answers were always, "I'm fine. I'm eating fine. I'm fine. No one's hurting me. Everything's fine."

Women who are incarcerated are not like men who are incarcerated. Women choose to form families. They choose to form alliances. Women form a sort of tribe with each other. There's a sisterhood and a feeling of *us versus them,* where "them" are the COs or the law. You develop relationships with the women. They call themselves your mother or aunt, your grandmother, your cousin, your sister.

When you do have a problem with someone you can fight it out, the two of you. It's not as if everyone's going to turn against you. It doesn't work like that unless you're a child molester. I was not being picked on or anything like that.

I did have to fight multiple times, but that comes with the territory of being incarcerated. It just happens. When that many women live together, they get sick of each other and so they fight. It's not so much of a bullying thing.

I was eating fine. I was getting commissary money. My mother was putting money on my "books," which is a way that you can put money toward an inmate. They can use that money to purchase things for themselves. It might be calling cards, hygiene items, clothes, shower shoes, whatever they need. I was doing fine. I was eating well. I was not in grave danger, other than with what you deal with every day—what becomes the norm.

That first visit was mainly about getting to know if I was alright. And he didn't just jump right into the whole "Jesus loves you" routine. It was a good 20 minutes of conversation about his son and his family before he went there.

That came when the visitation was wrapping up—the CO came over and said, "You've got five minutes." When we were leaving, that's when he told me that Jesus loves me. Then he asked, "Do you mind if I pray with you really quick?"

Everything in me was screaming, "NO!" but without thinking, I answered, "Sure." It was as if before I could even get out the word "no" my soul was calling out. And my answer was, "Yes, please. Will you pray for me?"

I can tell you that, honestly, I couldn't fight anymore. As much as I wanted to fight, I felt as though my soul was exhausted. My number was up.

I know myself. I know who I used to be. The old me would have screamed and cursed at that man and told him to get lost. I didn't need his prayers, and I didn't need his God. Yet, even with all of that in me wanting to say that, the word "yes" slipped out sooner than the thought of me saying "no."

So I can say that my soul cried out. It was no longer me. I look back now, and it's as though the "yes" leaped out of my mouth. I tried to push it back in, but it was too late. He was already seeing me.

Later I would learn that there was strength in my mother's prayer. It was her prayer that I would hear about God's love for me. That was the beginning of how I started to get a deeper understanding of how God works and how He is real.

He's *real*. It's not pretend.

God is real.

He put his hand up on the glass, and he said, "Scheila, can you put your forehead on the glass for me?"

I said, "Sure." I leaned my forehead close to the glass, and he put his hand up and he started to pray for me. He prayed that God would take my situation and turn it into *His* situation. And that was the end of the visit.

5

THIS IS REAL

I didn't know then, but I learned later on, that my mother had reached out to over 100 churches. *Over 100 churches* for somebody to come and see me. For somebody to come and bring me the Good News. For somebody to breathe life into me. And out of over 100 churches, only Pastor Jorge responded.

And when Pastor Jorge responded, he didn't just respond. He answered the call. He stood in the gap. The Bible talks about God asking, "Who'll stand in the gap?"

"I looked for someone among them who would build up the wall and stand before me in the gap on behalf of the land so I would not have to destroy it..." *Ezekiel 22:30* (NIV)

Only Pastor Jorge did that. He stood in the gap. My mother asked him to reach out to me and that's what he did.

In the process of hoping, I could see that God was already in the process of doing things. For the first time in my life, I could say that I actually started seeing things come about, out of my mother's faith. That things came about, out of my mother's person. That I could see the fruit that she was reaping.

I was in a bad spot then. But in the time when I was there with that pastor, it felt like I mattered for a moment. It felt like I was loved.

Sioni

Sometimes when I'm visiting with the women, they get a phone call and leave to take the call. When they come back, they tend to come back either very upset or very happy. Depending on the call, it could be good news; it could be bad news. When the news is bad and they are upset, I tell them, "You have no control over these things that happen on the outside. You can't do anything about it.

"You do have control over the things that happen here. *Learn things while you're incarcerated, then take it with you when you're out there.*

"Prepare your heart now. When you go out there, the same places and the same people will be there waiting for you. But you have to be ready to make the right choices."

⌘

There was a woman who came to the class but was angry and unhappy. Then without an apparent reason, one week she was a different human being. I don't know what happened, but she shared with me that she had goals for her life after her release from prison. She was going to go back to school to get her license to be a counselor. She wanted to help other people. She was completely positive!

She apologized to me for how she had been acting. She told me it was because things were terrible at home. A phone call would come, and she would have to deal with some bad situations. She reacted to these calls by acting out in class.

I was very encouraged to hear about her new attitude and the goals that she had. She became active in the class. She spoke candidly and shared many very good things.

One of the things she explained to the class was, "I used to sabotage relationships. I would hurt people before they hurt me."

Now she has changed the way she thinks. She had to do this, or the problems in her life would never change.

We have to make sure that we don't allow the devil to have a playground in our minds. Satan will lie to us so often that before we know it, we believe the ugly things we hear about ourselves. It's not the truth. The truth only comes from God.

She has been released but I don't know what she has done since then. I hope she fulfills her goals!

Scheila

There aren't a lot of positive days in prison. The day I'm remembering is mostly about shock and fear. It's not so much a sad day. It's more of a shocking day. An eye-opening day. It's a switching for me in my mind. It's when I finally realized where I was.

I had been incarcerated with someone who made news all throughout Washington state. She was a schoolteacher who was brought up on charges of molestation of one of her students. She actually was in the cell right next to mine. I would sometimes eat with her. Sometimes I prayed with her.

The pod I was put in was mixed with a lot of women who were older. I was one of about three young women there that did not have children.

Everyone else in the pod was a mother and many of the women I was incarcerated with had multiple children. I remember that much of the conversation would be them talking about their children. Some would draw pictures of their children and hang them up in their cell.

When I first walked into the pod, I was welcomed by a lot of the sisters there. My cellmate's name was Mama Snow. She introduced herself to me. She would become my mother figure when I was incarcerated. I noticed a woman there. She had short, light brown hair, kind of a red nose, red cheeks, big ol' blue eyes. She was a little on the heavier side, but she wasn't obese or anything. She was standoffish.

I noticed for the first couple of days when I got to the pod, that everyone seemed to isolate this woman. I would see the other inmates doing mean things to her, like tripping her, or bumping into her, or spitting on her. I even saw one woman go into her cell when she was in there by herself and start slapping her.

I didn't know for sure why they were treating her this way. I figured she had something to do with kids because that's their code of ethics. Believe it or not, there is a code of ethics when you're incarcerated. Some crimes are looked at as hated, some crimes are looked at as more wicked than others. We know that most of the time, crimes committed involve someone else who has also committed a crime. It's a cycle of crime on crime. But when children are involved, or weaker people are hurt or raped or molested or murdered, then it goes to another level.

Every time that she would walk around, people would say, "Rapist." "Disgusting." Anything possible to remind her every day what she was in there for. She pleaded and pleaded with everyone that she was not guilty.

One day, I was curious, so I asked her, "I need to know. Did you rape one of your students like they say?"

She said, "No. I didn't do this. They said I did this, but I would never do that. I have two young sons of my own. I'm married, I'm a Christian woman. I believe in God. I have faith in God." I often would see her reading her Bible.

When the time came, and she had gone to court, everyone was waiting for her to come back with the results. Everybody follows what everybody else has going on because there's not much else to spend your time on.

Before she came back from court, there was another woman in our pod who had gone to court that same day. She made an announcement. It wasn't only that her student was going to testify. Her sons came forward and said that she had molested them, as well.

I remember standing there. It was almost as if you could hear a pin drop. Everyone stopped what they were doing and looked at each other. Only about three people heard this news, but it was almost as if everyone sensed it. Everyone knew. We all stood there, looking at each other.

Some inmates who were mothers started to cry. They were so angry that tears started coming down their faces. I must have seen that on about eight faces. From women who might never see their children again. Women who would lose years of their child's life. Some women—who were looking at long sentences—had new babies before being incarcerated. There were women with children who would come and visit them. Some had teenagers, and they were missing out on the most important years of their lives. Some were looking at their kids going in a downward spiral as they made the same mistakes they had made. And there's nothing these mothers could do about it. Women cried about how they wished they could be with their babies. I knew so many of the women in the pod loved their children. One thought clicked in my head.

She's gonna die. Someone's gonna kill her. Somebody's gonna kill her when she walks in here.

Sure enough, there was a young woman nicknamed "Storm." She had also made headlines in Washington State. She had murdered her boyfriend. She did it by bludgeoning him in the head with a baseball bat while she was high on methamphetamines. She was a mother of two daughters. I remember hearing her say, "I'm gonna kill that b____."

I was angered, too because it's almost like a ripple effect. It's like everyone finds a common hate and everyone has the same enemy—there is no other enemy in the room. Everyone braced themselves for what they were preparing to do to her. Of course, I was young, so it was different. I'd been there long enough to know what was going on. But I didn't know the things that mothers could do to other people when children are mistreated.

It was in the daytime. The courts are usually in the morning. Everyone was waiting and lunchtime was coming up soon. Everything was normal, with people doing what they wanted to do. I was at the table playing pinochle which is a card game we played.

Storm came over, and she said to Momma Snow, "She should be back from court any minute now." She went around telling the women that were not only career criminals but who were also mothers. Mothers who loved their children, who adored their children. And she was going around whispering in everyone's ear. I said, "What's going on? What's the uproar all about?" But if there's one thing you learn in prison, it's that you don't ask questions. And that thing that you see, you pretend you don't see. And the things that you know, you pretend you don't know them.

Eventually, the door opened, and the guard shoved the schoolteacher in. She walked in with her paperwork, went into her cell and put her paperwork on her bunk. Six women got up, went into her cell and closed the door behind them.

There's a little window in the doors, and you can see right through them. The windows are small—just large enough for the guards to go by and see what you're doing. One of the women was standing up against the door leaning against the glass.

Everyone was looking around pretending that they weren't paying attention. They continued to work out or read their books, pretending to do whatever they were doing. But everyone was glancing around with their eyes. They were looking for the guards.

I got a glimpse through the glass and I could see hands flying. But I couldn't hear any sound from the cell. Everybody was making enough noise to muffle out any sound from behind that door. Everybody was loud and the TV volume was turned up extra high, but not so loud that it would draw a guard's attention. To an outsider, it would seem like nothing much was going on.

One by one, I saw the women come out. But the schoolteacher didn't come out. She didn't come out for lunch. And she didn't come out for dinner.

I used to work out in our pod, which would literally be us going around in a circle, fast-walking. We'd go up the stairs, do crunches and pushups. I'm one of those people who's always been very curious. So, as I was fast-walking past this door, I slowed down and peeked in. She was on the floor sobbing.

It looked like she was laying in wetness. Her hair was wet and everything she wore was wet. From what I had heard, they beat her up and had almost drowned her in the toilet. They believed that she didn't deserve to live anymore. They believed that she had done something so horrendous that there would be no mercy found for her—even among criminals.

COs come and check the pod when they do their count, sometimes only twice a day. Sometimes three times. It's up to each CO's discretion. You'll see a CO when it's chow time—breakfast, lunch, and dinner. But a CO's not going to go into each room to see if everyone's going to come out to eat. If you come out and eat, then you come out and eat. If not, that's on you. No one cares enough to make sure you're eating. The CO is only there to make sure that everything's fine. Some COs come in, open the door, survey the area from the doorway, and turn around to go out again. So, no one checked on the schoolteacher that day. She came out at her own discretion after dinner time. No CO found her from the span of before lunchtime until after dinner.

That day was a reality check for me.

This is serious stuff. I'm really locked up and I'm looking at a long time—I'm looking at 14 to 17 years. And this isn't even prison yet. This isn't the big house. This is only county jail.

I want to say that this also matured me in a way. It changed me because I didn't feel pity for her. I felt angered. I felt anger that she was crying. I felt anger that she was lying there playing the victim.

How could she be a victim? How could she think she's a victim? She's going around touching on kids, even her own kids.

I definitely wanted to do what everyone was doing, as a form of entertainment, as a way to pass the time. To feel something from it. But at the same time, I know that it wouldn't have affected me as much if I was by myself and she would have told me. I wouldn't have had so much anger towards her. But in a group setting like that, everyone gets so angry. It's almost as if everybody shares the same feelings.

Now that I'm older and God has come into my life, I've changed drastically. As a victim of sexual abuse, myself, I know that it is a chain that cannot be broken unless you have the necessary tools. I broke those chains and I thank God that He gave me the tools I needed. When I look at my daughter, I think of everything good I want to do for her. But that's only because my mind has been changed. It's been renewed. If I still had the same mindset of an abused person when I became a parent, I could have made my daughter a victim of abuse, as well. I know that now.

I don't know about the schoolteacher's childhood. We never had that conversation. But I know why she was scared out of her mind. She thought that anyone who got close to her would hurt her. I wonder how much hurt she had been through in her childhood. In her life. I wonder what made her do these things.

I look back on the women that were incarcerated for so many things.

What was it that had made them do those things? What made me do the things I did?

I remember my time of incarceration as being a time when I felt shocked. Maybe shell-shocked is a better description.

This is where I'm at. This is the stuff you see in a movie.

For the schoolteacher on that day, there were no guards around to stop the beating. They knew. But a lot of them thought she deserved what she got. No one came to help her. No one. Not even the women she ate lunch with. Not even the women who were in there for things that were not so great either. And that's the part that made me realize more than anything, that I was completely alone.

Whoa. So, this is where I'm at? Okay. This is real.

She never told anyone what happened that day. If you tell, the other inmates consider it snitching because you're going to seek the law. *We don't do the law. We don't welcome the law in our pod. We don't want anything to do with the law.* So, when you run and go to the law, you brand yourself. Being a snitch is worse than being a child molester. To save her own face, she did not tell anyone.

She was never that badly mistreated again after that day. But she was always mistreated. Any chance they got, they dropped water on her, or spit on her. Or anytime she'd walk by they'd say something or cut in front of her in line to get food or whatever.

⌘

Pastor Jorge's first visit happened in the time between my two confinements in the hole. When Pastor Jorge had been visiting me for some time, I started to read my Bible more. The schoolteacher always read her Bible. She would come up to me because she would see me reading mine. She showed me a method of reading the Bible that I sometimes still use. She would draw pink hearts on the word "love" in the Bible, and she would draw a purple cross over the word "peace." You could order colored pencils from the commissary. So, I ordered colored pencils, and I did the same in my Bible. It gave me comfort to be able to open my Bible and easily find passages of hope and peace when I needed them.

After Pastor Jorge first started visiting, hope was beginning to grow inside me again. That's when the second altercation happened. I look back on it now, being a believer and a Christian, and I realize that that was the devil. I look back now and I believe that the second fight happened after I started to be more at peace with the idea of serving God. I was more at peace with the idea that I was no longer in control of my life—that I'd *never* been in control of my life. That's when the fight happened. Looking back at it now, as a believer, I can say, *Oh yeah, that's got the devil written all over it.*

Pastor Jorge never gave up on me. I remember him particularly saying something about me in orange. When you go to the hole, they give you a new uniform. They dress you in all orange, which is a high alert so that everyone around knows that you're a high-risk inmate. And everywhere you go, you have to wear ankle cuffs. The ankle cuffs are connected to a long chain that connects to the handcuffs around your wrists. So everywhere you go, you're waddling, because the ankle cuffs don't give you much room.

I remember I walked in to see him, and I felt like I disappointed him. And he said something about why I was wearing orange. And I told him I had gotten into a fight. And he asked me if I was okay. He said, well, you look fine. And I said, "Yes, I'm fine." And he asked about what had happened to the other woman and I said, "I don't know. I'm sure she's okay."

Pastor Jorge never gave up on me.

He *never* gave up on me.

I don't think he'll ever know how much it meant to me that he kept coming. When I was in the hole, sometimes his was the only voice that I would hear for days, other than the CO bringing in my food tray. I don't think he'll ever understand how our conversation would replay over and over and over again in my mind.

He is the reason that I requested a Bible from the chaplain. He's also a reason why, when I was in the hole, I had carved bible verses into the wall. Everything he said to me stood out.

He would always talk to me about forgiveness, forgiving those who had hurt me, letting go of the anger. Every time I had a conversation with this man, it was almost as if he was looking into my soul.

I'd always leave there feeling dumb, questioning myself as if I didn't know who I was—because I didn't. He didn't see the same person as I did. He would see the real me. The "me" God had created but had been lost trying to find something else. But somehow, Pastor Jorge could see that the real me had been there all along.

I remember when he would visit me, he said, "You know, Scheila. One day you're going to look at this painful time, and God is going to use it to help people. And you're going to help people. God has a purpose for your life."

That made me laugh. *Who's ever going to want to listen to some ex-con talk about how they were locked up in a stinky prison cell? Who's gonna listen to that? Who's gonna want to hear anything I have to say?*

I figured that when I got out of prison, I was going to be the scum of society. But Pastor Jorge always reminded me that I wasn't. Instead, he said that when I got out, God was going to change my life. That God was going to send someone my way, and that I was going to go to his church. He was always speaking positiveness to me. He was always enforcing love and the idea that there was something so much bigger than the here and the now.

Pastor Jorge's visits made me hungry for more of the love he was projecting. The love that I could get from God… it made me hungry for more if it. Every time I'd get scared or lonely, I'd go to the Bible, and as soon as I saw a heart or a cross, I would start reading that verse. I figured that somewhere in there, something was going to inspire me, filled with the word *love* or the word *faith*.

6

SOME KIND OF RIGHTEOUSNESS

Sioni

About four years ago, I met a woman who was full of regret. She kept beating herself up. She was an alcoholic. She kept saying, "Even though I had this perfect marriage, I don't know what happened, but I became an alcoholic.

"I was a decent woman. I was a businesswoman. I had a husband; I had a family.   I loved my marriage and everything about it. But I became an alcoholic, and I lost everything.

"There were so many DUI violations that I ended up in jail."

Her frustration was that she had lived a normal life, but she had made the wrong choices. She got caught, and she ended up in the system. She was very regretful about it. She said, "I don't want to be here. I hate not being able to do anything. I feel worthless. I feel like I'm wasting my life."

And this is when I told her, "Sometimes we do things that aren't right. Don't beat yourself up about what you've done. The important thing is that you're moving forward.

"Don't look back into your past. Look up into your present. After you see the mistakes you made, now you move forward. It's never too late to start all over."

She was in prison for nine months. She told me about how she started communicating with her husband and her husband wanted her back! She told me, "I promise I will never come back here! I'm going to do something with my life. I hate this place. I'm going to change!"

I told her to shut the door of the past so that she could open the door to her future.

She got out. And I haven't seen her at the jail again!

Scheila

The schoolteacher and I started reading together sometimes. I prayed for her one time because she asked me to pray for her in court. I did pray for her. I remember that Pastor Jorge visiting me was starting to develop my sense of compassion.

I started to look at things the way Pastor would look at me, with the eyes of God. I started to realize that I was no better than anybody else there. I would show the schoolteacher that my Bible was completely covered in little symbols. I came up with my own symbols for words that were important to me, and we would discuss that.

Nothing changed between us after her beating. I knew what she was in there for. But I spoke with everyone a little. I made sure that I never got too close to anyone. It was nothing out of the ordinary that I started talking to her again. There was a group of individuals within the pod who spoke to everybody and never had any problems. They went around doing their own thing. They weren't concerned about other inmates. I was one of those people. I didn't care. So, it wasn't weird that I would talk to her, even though she was an outcast.

There were a couple of other women who spoke to her as well. Everyone kind of knows what everyone's in there for. If they don't know, they find out. Someone goes to court with you and finds out about your charges, or you might be in the newspaper or on the news. I was in the newspaper, so my picture showed up and everyone knew I was in for an armed robbery. When I got in there, everybody already knew my face before I even got to the pods. Everybody already knew I wasn't a child molester or anything like that.

I never sat back and thought about myself as any kind of righteous person. I considered myself dumb. In fact, I took pride in being a lowlife. Righteousness was the furthest thing from my mind.

There was so much anger. Anger to victimize the next person without calling it victimization. It's a cycle of a victim no longer wanting to be a victim. A large portion of the women who are incarcerated are victims of some kind of sexual violence. Many women have told me endless stories about what happened to them when they were younger. They might think, in the moment, that somehow, they could find retribution for what was done to them. I'm a victim of sexual abuse. I wanted to hurt this schoolteacher who hurt those children. I did. I wanted to do horrible things to her. Did I ever think about that before? No. It was never presented in front of me as *here's someone who molested somebody like you were molested.*

But when you're incarcerated, you learn that the devil is real. And every demon you could imagine is hidden deep inside. All that is going to come out. You have to face every last one of them because you have nothing but time and your thoughts. That's all you have.

The mindset you have when you're incarcerated is not a "free" mindset. You're in there for a crime, for hurting someone, for making someone a victim, or taking from someone. Yet somehow you think you have some kind of righteousness over the next person.

It isn't until you come to God that you realize that not one of us is righteous. Not one. When a person is incarcerated, it's more than their body that's in jail. Their thinking is not free, and they're locked up mentally.

But God can liberate your mind, even when you are incarcerated. God has the ability to change our minds; the ability to change our whole structure and the way we think. We might assume that we are all victims. That if we keep committing crimes on other victims, that we somehow will no longer be victims ourselves. It's a cycle. And that cycle will never be broken unless we allow God to come to break it. And only He can.

The story of what happened to the schoolteacher is a reminder to me every day. It reminds me that you're wrong if you think you are more righteous than the next person. Really, none of us is righteous. Our righteousness comes from the glory of Christ.

I've begged God to change my mind from wrong thinking. He sometimes reminds me of the schoolteacher. And He reminds me of how wrong it was, even for a second, to think I was better than her.

If I could go back to that time, I would say something to her when she was on the floor, sobbing. I would explain what I've learned. Nothing lasts forever. Pain is a reminder, sometimes, that you're still alive even while you're going through it. I know because I went through a lot of pain when I was incarcerated, a lot of mental torment. I went through physical pain. I went through horrible, horrible things. And I had to remind myself that this was not going to be forever. It was only in that particular moment.

I didn't have a mindset on God or set on the bigger picture. My mind was always set on the things going on around me. It wasn't until I started getting a little more knowledge of God that I was able to understand things beyond me. Things above me, around me, inside of me. I changed. My eyes were opened. I started to understand the more important things—the things that matter. The things that bring eternal peace.

The noise around you or the things that surround you don't really matter. None of that matters. God has a way of silencing all hate and reminding you and holding you and telling you it's going to be okay. God's plan and His purpose for our lives? Nothing is going to deter that. Nothing is going to stop the path that we were meant to serve Him on. Nothing. We should remind ourselves that this is for right now, but the greater plan is still ahead.

Sioni

Amelia was a petite lady, in her mid-sixties. She had very long hair, and she usually wore it down when she came to class. She would sit on my right, two chairs down. She was quiet at the beginning, and very soft-spoken.

One time I approached her to try to draw her into a conversation.

"Hi, Amelia. How're you feeling today, on a scale of 1 to 10?"

"I'm okay. I would say I'm a '6'." Every time she talked, she looked down, and she wrote things in her notebook.

After some time, she got comfortable enough to start looking me in the eye and to talk to me. It became clear to me that she was intelligent and well educated. She shared with me that she came from very wealthy people. She and her husband had owned their own business.

But money doesn't guarantee happiness. The couple was always fighting. They argued over things like her husband's spending habits. She would get angry about how quickly he ran through money. They had so much money that he wasn't worried about lavish spending. He would go ahead and buy whatever he wanted without thinking about it.

She said that one day they started with some drugs. At first, it was a curiosity. They wondered what it would be like. And they had enough money to afford it. $500 a day was nothing between her and her husband.

I could see from her red eyes that she was about to cry. I could see the pain was deep inside her heart. She wasn't bragging about how much money she had. She was concerned about her husband.

I made eye contact with her and said, "Life is like a wheel. You're here one day, and somewhere else the next. You're going to make choices about the direction you move in. You may or may not like where you end up. But you have to appreciate the wheel for getting you there."

She seemed to feel safe and continued to come to the class every week. I could see her smiling more and she opened up more often. She became a mentor for some of the younger girls. They all went to her when they had questions.

Once I asked the ladies if they wanted to share something about what they had done in their life that they regretted. Immediately she started crying. That was the first time I had seen her break down that way. It was plain to see the pain in her eyes.

She said, "I know God has a plan in my life and I know why I'm here."

Amelia is a mature lady, so it's not like she was naive. She understood that choices have consequences. Just before she was arrested, she figured out that whatever she was doing; it wasn't fulfilling her needs. She got tired of that lifestyle. Whatever she was doing was getting her into so much trouble that before she was arrested, she decided to give up the drugs.

She told us about her surrender that day. She told us she prayed, "God—have Your will with my life."

She said, "Sioni, two days later, I'm here in this place. If I hadn't been caught, maybe I would be dead by now." She felt that being in jail had saved her life.

She and her husband lost everything because of the drugs they used, and the debts they incurred. But just when she was at her lowest point, she decided to change her life. She wanted to start over again. She was hungry to get more from her life.

It seemed like it was the end of her days when she turned her life around. I could see that she was doing it because she wanted to change her life. Of course, they lost all their business. They lost everything because of the drugs and the debts that they both have. But she wanted to start a new life.

She shared with me that she wanted to retire to Costa Rica. She said, "I want to live my life in peace. I know I can find peace in that country."

I said, "How do you know that?"

She said, "I went up there a couple of years ago and I fell in love with that country. And that's where I want to go when I retire."

She knew that I grew up in Costa Rica. She told me about some places she went to and I could say, "Oh yeah. I know that place!"

Living in peace was her goal.

When you have goals in life, you can begin to look forward. You can say, "I'm going do something. When I get out of here, I can make choices that will make my life better."

Amelia got a wake-up call. Now she's got a goal. She's moving forward.

Scheila

Pastor Jorge would talk to me as if he were talking to me now. He would talk to me as if I already understood. He smothered me in love.

I feel almost as though his eyes were mirrored. He would tell me things like, "I know you're scared. I know you're angry. I *know*."

That used to be his key phrase. "I *know*."

He also said, "I'm praying for you."

Every conversation we had, he would tell me he was praying for me five or six times. Sometimes people say, "I'm praying for you," but you say to yourself, O*h, you're not praying for me. You're just saying that.*

I believe that when this man said he was praying for me, that he *was* praying for me. He was. It drove me to read my Bible a lot more. His prayers for me, drive me to pray for women who are incarcerated as I was.

I want you, the reader who is imprisoned or the families that love them, to know that I'm praying for you now.

This is absolutely real.

Father,

I know I have let You down. I know who I am now in You. You have opened my eyes, filled my soul with everything I was looking for.

I pray, Father, that You open the eyes of those reading this. That You remind them of the crowns placed on their heads.

Remind them of the strength You have buried deep within them.

Comfort them. Cradle them in Your arms.

Whisper in their ears that they are not forgotten, and they never will be.

Satisfy the questions and sadness weighing them down. Life has been hard, Father, and times have been dark. But You have always carried the light. Burn that fire inside of us all.

Awaken our true selves.

Let us stare in the mirror and love what we see.

All our brokenness... all our pain... is a jewel crafted in the crown of life we wear.

I pray you find your true self and learn to love yourself as much as your Father in heaven loves you. I pray you come to a deeper understanding and embrace the cards you have been dealt.

I love you and I know what you can do with your life! Don't let the devil imprison your mind or your soul!

You are a fire, a fighter, a lioness and loved—so deeply loved!

" 7 "

CHOICES

When I was initially booked, I went before a judge for the first time for an arraignment hearing. This is when your charges are given to you and you learn what punishment you might receive if proven guilty. The prosecutor informed me that I was facing 14 to 17 years.

I felt total despair at the idea of being incarcerated for the next 14 years of my life. But as the process continued, I was offered a deal. If I pled guilty to the charges, my sentence would be lowered to seven years.

But then the final deal came to the table. The prosecutor told me, "sign this or we're going to trial. If you go to trial and are found guilty, without a shadow of a doubt, your sentence will be maxed out and you'll get 14 years." He said, "Plead out now. We'll go down to five years."

I protested, "Wait. Five years is still a long time!"

I was 18. Five years feels like forever when you're 18. Then again, five years feels like forever no matter what your age. Five years *is* a long time when you know you're going to be sitting in jail day after day.

My lawyer was persistent, but I needed to think about this. My mother would call and give me advice. She would tell me things like, "No. Don't take it yet. It's not God's timing. Don't take it yet."

I talked to my lawyer one last time, and he said, "Okay, I'll go again to the prosecutor and see if we can get three years." I'm thinking, *Okay. This looks positive. I can do three years.*

I remember calling my mother and saying, "Hey, Mom. The prosecutor agreed to three years. The lawyer's telling me this is it, Mom. If I don't sign this, I'm gonna go to trial and they'll find me guilty." I knew this because I did it. I committed a crime. I hurt someone. I made someone a victim with my anger, and I needed to pay for that. I knew there wasn't going to be any kind of leniency toward me because of the violence of the crime.

Inexplicably, my mother disagreed, "No, Baby. Don't plead guilty. You're not getting three years. You're not getting two years. God's not going to let you sit in there for even a year and a half. You're going to get out in less than a year."

I remember saying, "Less than a year? I've already been sitting in county jail for almost six months. What is she talking about?" And in a way, it would anger me... all her positivity.

At the same time, I couldn't get enough of it. There was this weird thing I had going on in my mind all the time. I was numb from pain, yet I was getting hope breathed into me. It was like a wilted flower sitting in the rain. I gave in to her.

Okay. Whatever.

I was already reading my Bible somewhat. Was I born again? Had I dedicated my life to God? Was I making the changes in my soul that I had to make? No. Faith was not completely grounded in my heart yet. The idea of being released didn't click. Still, mom would say, "I'm praying for you, Baby. God's not going to let you sit in there long."

My attorney came to me. "I spoke to your mom."

My mom was in constant contact with my attorney throughout the whole time I was incarcerated. She would call him; they would call each other.

He told me about their last call. This time she told him, "My daughter's not going to sit in that jail. My God is not going to let my daughter sit in there.

He told me He's got a purpose for her life, and He's going to get her out."

The attorney, explaining this to me, was kind of laughing it off. He said, "We have to be realists. We have to know that, yes, it's a good idea that God is going to get you out, but that's not going to happen. You're going to sign the plea, and you're going to go away for three years."

I was taken back to the holding area and a couple of hours later my lawyer called me. "Hey. I'm coming up to see you. I'm going to talk to the prosecutor about your deal, and when I'm done, I'll be there."

In jail, there's a lawyer/client phone. It's separate from the other phones that you can use your calling card on. This one was a blue phone, and it was set apart, only to be used by lawyers to call their inmate clients. When that phone rings, any inmate can pick it up, and the lawyer will say, "Yeah. Can you please put inmate so-and-so on the phone?"

That phone rang for me a few hours later, and he said, "Miss Jimenez, I'm coming to see you." He hung up the phone so fast, that I knew.

Okay. I'd better be ready to go on the Purdy train (named for the state women's prison). He's going to come, and he's bringing the documents. He's going to tell me to sign here, this is your plea agreement.

I was almost okay with it. I had actually become comfortable with the idea of being incarcerated. I had adapted to the lifestyle. I found a way to survive.

The room for the lawyers to meet with their clients is stark. It has a white desk and there's a big padded chair where your lawyer sits. Inmates get a little, plain, plastic chair with metal legs.

They brought me to the room, and my lawyer was already there, sitting, waiting for me.

They closed the door and my lawyer began.

"I don't know how to explain it. I don't know what happened. But someone upstairs favors you, *and you are the apple of His eye.*"

He continued. "The prosecutor said he'll give you a year and a day."

I couldn't believe it. I thought I was dreaming. I thought somebody was going to wake me up soon and I would have to go in and get lunch or something.

Everything stopped.

I'm looking at this man, and he's still talking, but no words are coming out of his mouth. I'm looking at the paper and the words are all jumbled, and it all looks like one big word.

FREEDOM!

That's all I heard. Freedom. I didn't hear anything else he said. I didn't hear, "The prosecutor said the victims aren't coming to testify. One victim isn't coming, they can't find him. He disappeared, and he wants nothing to do with this. There's no reason as to why." Still stunned, I signed the document!

I signed it and the first thing I did was to go back to my cell. Everybody had the same question, "What's going on?" "What happened?"

"I'm getting out. I'm getting out."

That's all I could say. I immediately went to my bunk and grabbed my phone card and I called my Mom. We sobbed together on the phone. She said, "I told you, Baby. I told you. You've got to have faith." She told me, "God showed me. He told me. He assured me that you weren't going to sit there locked up."

I was ecstatic. I don't want to say I was a true believer, because I still wasn't yet. But I believed one thing. I knew for sure.

This... this God is real. This God that my mother serves... He's the real God.

Things started to happen. I got to know this God. I got to know His power. To think that not a whole justice system could stop Him from saying, "Hey! You're not going to take her because I'm going to use her."

And that's what I couldn't fathom. I started to think about how He noticed me. And why He would even consider moving these mountains in my life. I never thought of myself as anything. I never saw myself as a child of God. I never saw myself as a new creation. I never thought that one day God would use me.

I got credit for the time I already served. For each day that I was in county jail, I got a day counted toward my time. With a sentence of a year and a day, that didn't leave me with a lot of time left.

I really was happy to know that I was getting released. But I also started falling into a bad depression and despair. I started wondering what I was going to do when I got out, and how I didn't have anyone in Washington state to help me.

⌘

Part of my plea agreement was that to get out early, I had to be on probation for three years. I would have to report to a probation officer whenever the probation officer wanted to see me. It could be every week or whenever. Either way, I had to have an address in the state of Washington.

My family was all on the east coast. I had literally nowhere to go. I had no home. I had no address. I had no family physically there. I had nothing materially.

God used this problem to teach me. I know it was God. God gave me somewhere to stay. He gave me the means to survive.

The girlfriend of my codefendant was a very good friend of mine. When we were released, she was there to pick up both of us. I had formed a friendship with another inmate. She was there to pick me up as well. So, I had somewhere to stay right from when I was released.

But I was going back to the mess that got me in jail in the first place. I was going back to the same environment. I was going back to the same life. It was sad.

I started to think about the idea that I was going to be released. About the environment I was going to be released back to. It was frightening. I was scared because I didn't know what I was going to do when I got out. I had nothing. I was going to be released with a bag of toiletries from the jail, my documents from the court, and the clothes on my back. They didn't even give me back the clothes I initially got booked in with. Those clothes were being kept as evidence, so they had to give me borrowed clothes.

I had nothing. I had no one. I was all alone again.

I felt abandoned by God again.

You saved me and You got me released and You did all this. But what did You release me back in to?

I started to blame Him for the deal where I had to go on probation for three years. I asked my probation officer many times if they could move my probation to New Jersey where my family was. But they wouldn't. The state wouldn't allow it.

So, yes, my release was good news, and I was very happy. But at the same time, it was frightening because I was going back into the same world of sadness and despair.

When I was released, someone else was there to pick me up that day. Pastor Jorge was there. Pastor Jorge hugged me, and he was so happy to see me, and I was happy to see him. At the same time, the other two girls who came to pick me up were hugging me and happy to see me.

And they all looked at me as if to say, *Where are we going?*

I remember looking at Pastor Jorge and saying, "Pastor Jorge, I'm going to go with them."

The look on the man's face... he pleaded with me. He said, "No, Scheila, come with me. My wife, she wants to see you. Let's go get something to eat." It's like he knew. Of course, he knew.

Still... still, I chose to do my own thing. To go my own way. It was as though the miracles that God made in my life counted as nothing. It was forgotten in an instant when faced again with the world, and I couldn't go with him.

I hated myself as I walked away. And I hated how much of a traitor I had been to him. And how besides my family, he was the only one who stood by me. And I turned my back on him.

⌘

There was something important that I didn't understand until after I began my walk with God in earnest. I had done the same thing to Christ as I did to Pastor Jorge.

I turn my back on God every time I commit a sin, every time I go against what He wants. Every time I give in to my own desires, it's like I'm doing it to Pastor Jorge all over again. It's like I'm walking away from Christ. And in my mind, I'm looking back at Him and He's standing there beside His car and He's waiting. Waiting. And He's letting me know, *I'll be here when you come back. I'll be here when you're done. I'm never going away. I'll always want the best for you.*

I had the choice right there. It was handed to me the minute I was released. The minute I was released, everything good was handed to me. A second opportunity. An opportunity to go to church. The opportunity to live with a family who would have loved me and taken care of me. Would have helped me get a job. Would have helped me get on track.

But then there was this group of individuals that I thought knew me. They owned me. I wasn't enlightened yet. I *thought* I was and so I gave in to the urges.

Go with them, hang out for a little bit. You miss them and it's been a long time. You're free now. Let's have fun!

Sometimes, when we're faced with decisions, we go with the known instead of the unknown. It's what we're used to. We'd rather know what our life is going to be like, even if it's bad. That's because the other option means going into the unknown, even if we know there's a chance that it'll be good. Because we're scared of change.

What are they going to expect of me? What am I going to have to do?

There were two things that were going on in my mind. I was free, and I was desperate to keep that freedom. But I didn't come to realize until later on, that I was never free until I was awakened, and I became a new person in Christ. This was a false freedom. I was back in the same place I was when I got locked up.

I got in their car and we drove off.

And I looked back through the glass, and Pastor Jorge was still standing there by his car. He had given me his number, and he told me to call if there was anything, anything he could do to help me. If anything went wrong. If I needed him for anything. "I don't care what time it is." I took the paper and slipped it in my back pocket.

And that night I partied all night long. I partied, and I did all kinds of horrendous things that night, trying to make up for the time I had lost.

I think about that now, sometimes. I think about how so many times we're faced with that predicament. Faced with the choice of going with our urges and old habits or going with what we *know* is right. I knew going with Pastor Jorge was the right thing to do. I *knew* it was. But I didn't want to because I wanted to do what I wanted to do, which was to give in to my own desires. I think about that a lot.

I also think about how Pastor Jorge, once again, played almost a Jesus role in my life. When I walked away from him, he was still there waiting.

I think of the story of "The Prodigal Son", and how we can squander everything that God has given us. But still, His merciful arms are always waiting for us to come running back. There's nothing we could do to change this. I think about that all the time. That even though the devil won that moment—and he did—I didn't realize the strength and the power that I had. I didn't realize that God had already equipped me with all I needed to extinguish the devil at that moment.

I didn't know what I know today. That will always be a fight that the devil won that day. But going forward, a lot of things changed. I did go to Pastor Jorge's church.

And I did eventually go to a church where I gave my life to God. I went to the altar, and I wept my heart out. And when I got up, I was never the same. I think about that a lot these days.

Now I understand what God expects. It's that you strip yourself and see who you really are and acknowledge how much you need Him. That's the only thing that's expected of you when you come to God.

I may have been physically released from prison, but at first, my mind was still confined. I had taken on mannerisms as though I was still locked up. I still looked around a lot, making sure nobody was around the next corner. I became paranoid. There were several things going on with me. When I was released, I had this oddity, this tick. I haven't gotten rid of it, actually. Sometimes my knee starts to shake uncontrollably when I'm sitting still. I didn't have that before I was incarcerated.

And my mind wasn't in the same place as it was before. I did realize that I was given a choice. I knew that I would have to make this choice because of the way God had worked in me. The way God had done so much, I knew a lot was going to be required of me. It's not that God is like one of those people who say, "I did something for you. Now you do something for me." That's not it.

When you're raising your child, one of the things you do is to practice the alphabet with your child. If you do this every day, by the time they go to kindergarten, they will know their alphabet. It's going to be required of them. You're prepping your child for what you already know they're going to need. I believe that God was doing that with me. When I was incarcerated, He was prepping me for what I was going to face.

The problem is, so was the devil.

Unfortunately, I did not have the knowledge that I have now to have seen it for what it was. Where I could say, "Not today, Satan. Those days are over. I'm not going back to that. I'm going with this pastor, and that's something you're going to have to deal with until the day I die."

But I didn't have that knowledge then. I went back to my street life, and I ended up going to prison again for a probation violation.

The knowledge I have now led me from homelessness. It led me from sleeping at multiple people's houses, from couch hopping.

Eventually, I was able to work on what it means to be loved by God, to where He was able to really save me.

" 8 "

HE PRAYED ALL NIGHT LONG

I partied the whole night, that first night after I was released. I remember feeling so lost. I looked around and there was a room full of people lying on the beds... lying on the floor... sideways... everybody passed out on the floor wherever they were. Everybody was in their own drug-induced, alcohol-induced comas. They fell asleep wherever they were sitting or standing. There were people leaning up against the wall, asleep.

And I remember, in a room full of about ten people, I felt so alone.

I was stricken with guilt and sadness. I felt so... I felt gross. I felt so dirty. I felt so... wrong. I knew what I had done was wrong.

The old me never thought like that. The old me never thought what I did was wrong. It didn't matter what it was. I always had a reason for what I said or what I did. But lying in this bed, on the edge and looking up... looking around at everything... I felt so alone.

I didn't feel that hope in my heart that I felt when I was reading my Bible or praying or visiting with Pastor Jorge. This feeling was a different feeling, yet at the same time a very familiar feeling. A feeling I had felt so many times before. The feeling you feel when you've exhausted your body. When you've exhausted your soul... your mind.

So empty.

I got up, and I started looking for my paperwork and the book my mother had given me when I was in jail. Then I found Pastor Jorge's number in my jeans. The book my mother had given me is called *The Purpose Driven Life.*[1] I tucked the paper with his number between the pages of this book.

Later, I looked for the paper. I couldn't find it. I started feeling almost desperate, and I started looking everywhere. Someone woke up; I don't remember who it was.

"What are you looking for?"

---

[1] Warren, Rick. *The Purpose Driven Life: What on Earth Am I Here for.* Zondervan, 2002.

"I'm looking for a phone number." And in all my panic I woke everybody up. I continued to look until I went back to the book again. The number was there, stuck between the pages the whole time.

I believe that not being able to find Pastor Jorge's number was a mind trick from the devil. It was just one more game with my heart, one more game with my feelings, one more moment where I felt I was losing my mind.

⌘

After I found the number in the book, I called Pastor Jorge.

"Pastor Jorge? I'm at this hotel. I just wanted to call you."

"Oh, Scheila! I was praying for you all night long!"

I knew he was telling me the truth. The night after I was released—that night when I was partying—I was doing drugs that I hadn't done before. On top of that, I was drinking a lot. To look back on it, I could have overdosed. It had been a long time since I had done some drugs or drank alcohol, but I did it anyway.

It was bad. It was like black-out bad. I think to myself now that the reason I did it was that I felt so guilty. The fact that I wasn't where I was supposed to be. That I wasn't doing what I know God wanted me to do.

And I called him, and he said, "I was praying for you last night."

I said, "Oh, Pastor Jorge, I know you were."

He said, "What are you doing today?"

"Well, the next step is to try to find a job. I've got to go talk to my probation officer. And I've got to look for a job."

That morning, I reported to my probation officer for the first time. I would report there for the remainder of the next three years. My probation officer gave me a piece of paper with businesses that might be hiring. Places that were felon-friendly.

I called every employer and none of them had any positions available. I was willing to apply anywhere, but no one wanted to hire me. No one wanted to help me. So, I went back to doing what I had done before.

Since the moment I left prison, everything was in a downward spiral. It got to the point where I didn't have a home. I didn't have anywhere to stay.

I was on probation, so it was mandatory for me to report every week and to provide an address. But I didn't have my family there. I didn't have anyone; I didn't have anything. The people that I ended up staying with the night I was released from jail let me stay with them for a while.

Then I was living on the street. It got very bad for me, to the point where I was doing anything possible to survive. If that required me to hurt someone, I would do it. If it required me to steal from someone innocent, or if it required using means of violence, I did it. It was like that for a long time.

I met up with an old friend of mine, and I ended up staying with her. She was house hopping as well. She was living on the streets. We became a pair. We eventually met up with another of her female friends. We became a household of women who were just trying to survive. That is until God gave me the wake-up call I really needed.

I experienced first-hand the persistence of how God works. I was incarcerated for the second time for a probation violation. I was staying in the house with the two other women. This was the house address that I had listed with my probation officer. My probation officer made a surprise visit.

She came to the house, and she found a weapon under the couch. As a felon, I'm not supposed to be anywhere near weapons. I was arrested because of that and I was immediately sent to prison.

It was like that for a long time before there was any hope. Any light. It had gotten very dark for me.

⌘

When I was released the second time, my father came to visit me in Washington. He had made very good friends with a Mexican woman who was married. She had a 15-year-old daughter who she said was out of control and needed some guidance.

My father said, "My daughter is in prison, but she's changing her life. Maybe she can come to stay with you until I come and get her, or she has the means to come back to New Jersey on her own." The woman said, "Of course! She can stay with me." What happened next would prove to me that God was in this arrangement.

One Saturday morning I was outside on the front porch, smoking a cigarette. Two people walked up to the gate, a woman and a man. Later I learned that their names were Amy and Kenny. They walked up to the gate and said, "Hello. We're from the Christian church in this area, and we're out inviting people to come to church with us on Sunday."

I went up to the fence. It was like the first time I met Pastor Jorge. He asked me if he could pray for me, and I told him *yes*, even though everything in me wanted to say *no.* Here again, before I could tell them that I wasn't interested, those same words came out of my mouth.

"Yes. Absolutely."

I tried to push the words back in, but I couldn't. The look on these people's faces... It was almost as though they had already known what I would answer.

Later on, when I would serve God and I would go to church almost daily, they would tell me their side of the story. They were out knocking on doors, inviting people to go to church. They were sitting in their car, and they had seen me on the porch. They prayed for me before they even came up to the fence.

They prayed that they could provide whatever it was that I needed. They prayed that God would use them to take me to the place where I needed to be to receive it. This place would be their church where I would hear His Word again.

Sioni

I remember Alejandra. She was a tall, pretty girl who came to the class. The first thing she did was to sit down and throw her legs over the chair. She crossed her arms and looked around with an angry stare. It was obvious to me that even though she was checking us out, she wasn't going to be a push-over.

I'm glad that I never tell them what to do. My goal is to have them in the class. It doesn't matter to me whether they're writing a note, or playing with a pencil, or drawing a picture, or paying attention to me. I don't care. I just want them to be there. I didn't say anything to her.

There was another girl in the class who Alejandra did not like. Alejandra said that if this girl was going to be in class, that she wouldn't come. The following Sunday, Alejandra came to the door but stopped when she saw the girl was there.

"No. I'm not coming in. Not if she's here. I'm out of here!"

I looked at her and I said, "Listen. If I tell you a joke, and you laugh, would you stay in the class?"

She was suspicious, but she agreed.

I was worried. What joke could I tell that would make her laugh? Finally, I told her a joke that my husband had told to me.

"What do you call a Spanish man with a rubber toe?" They looked at me, confused. I repeated the question. They indicated that they didn't know.

"Roberto!"

Everyone in the class was laughing except her.

She glared at me and said, "That's not funny."

"Oh, you don't think that's funny?"

"No. My son's name is Robertito!"

I apologized right away. "I'm so sorry! Listen. Just stay. Just stay today. I promise you; you will not regret it."

She said, "You know why I don't want to stay? Because that girl is here."

I pulled her to the side, and I let the other girls talk among themselves. I told her, "You know, you have such great potential. You've answered some questions here, and you seem like such a smart woman. Please don't leave. Don't pay any attention to these girls. I'd love for you to be the example here."

I started to speak to her in Spanish—nice things, some encouraging words for her. She said, "Okay. I'll stay."

Even though it wasn't always easy, I'm glad that I never turned Alejandra away, or made her take a seat with her legs down. She stayed in the class for almost a year. And by the time she left the jail, Alejandra would talk. Not in an angry way. But in a kind and respectful way.

Scheila

Kenny said, "We'll come back tomorrow morning, we can pick you up."

I said, "Sure. That's fine. Yeah."

The next morning, there they were... knocking on the door. I looked out cautiously, and I remembered Amy. I said, "Oh. Hey. Never mind. I can't come." She almost put her foot in the door.

"Wait! What do you mean you can't come? C'mon. Get dressed!"

"I don't have anything to wear to church."

She said, "Oh, it doesn't matter. Wear whatever. Wear what you're wearing."

At that point, nobody was at home, so I said, "Nobody's home so I'd better wait for somebody to get home." As soon as I said that, the woman and the man that I was staying with were coming home and their car hit the corner.

Everything I tried to say, every wrench I tried to throw, didn't deter them.

"Oh, I don't feel good, I've got a headache." She popped out a bottle of aspirin, and said, "Don't worry. I've got some pain pills right here!"

It was my time. My number was up, and God had the last word. *Listen. That's it. It's time to collect. You've got to come to church. You've been out there long enough. It's time to come home, Daughter. It's time to come home.*

They persisted and persisted until finally, I said, "Okay. Let's go. Let's just go."

They put me in the car, and they talked to me. They tried to make me feel comfortable. They were looking at me as if they were thinking that I must have gone through some bad stuff. I knew they could see it was so. Later I found out that they were scared to even approach the fence because I looked so angry. They thought that I was going to… I don't know… hit them! That's crazy! They said that God had told them, "Keep going. Keep going. She needs to come."

And later, I developed a very good friendship with Amy. She would come to tell me that God had laid it on her heart, "You cannot leave here without taking her with you."

I don't know if it was because something was going to happen. There are so many questions I have for God when I meet Him. But God was right. He was ready for things to start happening. He was ready for lives to get touched. He was ready for my story to be told because the time was coming when people needed to hear about Him. Where we needed to know more about HIs love for us and His mercy, and about what He could do in people's lives.

So, as we were driving to the church, and I was in the back seat, I remember looking out the window and looking up to the stars.

God, I know my mind, and my body, and my soul want me to turn around. But I don't have strength left in me these days. I haven't felt it in a long time. You released me from prison that one time, but I never saw You again. If You're real, then make Yourself known to me. Let me know You're real.

There's something we say on the streets, "Keep it real." That means don't lie to me. Don't sugarcoat things. Tell me 100% how it is so everything's on the table.

God—keep it real with me. I need to know if You're real. This is something I need to know.

And even I knew who He was because I knew what He had done through the faith of my mother. I knew He was real.

But I still had doubts because I hadn't had that personal one-on-one with Him. This was something that was in answer to my mother's prayer. It favored me because she prayed for me. But I hadn't had that piercing moment where it's just you and God, standing there, and nobody's between you.

I got to the church. It was a humongous church. And I saw all these people ushering in the crowd and they're dressed so nicely. And I looked at myself and how I came to church in jeans and a t-shirt. I started to feel so bad about myself. I started to get all these feelings again about loneliness.

But when I walked into the church, I was overcome with *Welcome!* People were there at the door greeting. A woman hugged me and said, "Welcome! Welcome! It's so good to see you!" Everybody was so happy. Everybody was so filled with love. It was like there was a bunch of Pastor Jorges running around! I felt like these people had gotten what he had! They did the same things. They all had the same Word!

I got up to the church. I sat down. The music started. I clapped. I was clapping awkwardly because I saw people who got really excited singing these songs. I'd never seen people get so excited about singing songs. They were jumping up and down and there was light everywhere. Everything looked so clean and everyone was so happy. Everyone was so happy to be there together.

Sioni

Vivian used to come every week, but she would cry a lot in class.

She and her daughter hadn't spoken for many years. Her daughter had children, and she wasn't allowed to see her grandchildren. Every time she came to class, she cried about it. She was sad because she couldn't connect with her daughter, and that her daughter would never forgive her.

One time I spoke on the subject of forgiveness. She told me, "I'm so ready to forgive, but my daughter won't forgive me."

A couple of months went by. Vivian kept coming to the class, and she was very receiving about what was said in class.

One day she came with this big smile. She sat down, and I asked her why she was smiling. "You look very happy!"

She said, "Well, I feel almost like a number 10 today!"

"Woo-hoo! Do you want to share with the class about what's changed?"

She said, "My daughter is here!"

Vivian's daughter ended up in prison. And because her daughter didn't have anybody else, she started talking to Vivian. She eventually forgave her mother. They restored their relationship while they were still in prison.

It was clear that Vivian cherished her daughter, so I told her, "You've been talking about your daughter, and so I want to meet her."

Vivian wasn't sure that she wanted to come to the class. I said, "Invite her!"

Her daughter came the next week. I soon found out she had a beautiful singing voice, and so I asked her, "Would I put you on the spot if I asked you to sing a song for me?"

She said, "I don't know any Christian songs."

"It doesn't matter. Sing any song. I just want to hear your voice."

Her mother's eyes were melting with love for her daughter.

The song she picked to sing? "Amazing Grace!"

Her voice was beautiful, like an angel.

"Amazing Grace, How sweet the sound
That saved a wretch like me.
I once was lost, but now am found
T'was blind but now I see."

⌘

Another woman who came to my class had four daughters, and she came to prison pregnant with daughter number five. I remember how I remarked that she had four beautiful babies. She was depressed, though, because they were taking her children away into foster care.

Then one day she wasn't as down as she normally would be.

"You're happy today!"

She said, "I'm happy today because I'm at peace."

"That's a great way to be when you feel a peace about things. Why are you at peace?"

"My children got fostered, and they moved to Florida," she explained. It turns out that she had been worried because she thought the girls would be split into different homes. But she learned that they kept all four together.

"I feel so happy because the person that is going to adopt is willing to adopt all four girls!"

She left the prison after her fifth daughter had been born. A couple of months later, I learned that she was going to be visiting my church for an event. I got word to her that I would be at the service and wanted to see her. She didn't show up at that event, but she did make it on a different night when I wasn't there. Although she left word for me that she was looking for me, I never did see her again. But I like to think that she found her way to a good church and made a safe home for herself and her baby girl.

" 9 "

THE APPLE OF HIS EYE

Scheila

Finally, we sat down, and the pastor got up to speak. Later, he would become my pastor. This man would become the second most important spiritual guide in my life, next to Pastor Jorge. His name was Pastor Kinson. He began to preach a message entitled: *Rebuilding That Once Which We Destroyed.* I remember the title to this day. I remember every word that came out of that man's mouth.

Pastor Kinson was almost like a Southern preacher, and he used his hands a lot. He was filled with the Spirit and he really *preached*. That man would almost scream into the mic and pointed his finger for emphasis. I was in a crowd of about 500 people. But it seemed like the whole time he was preaching that he was pointing his finger right at me.

He said, "The Lord knows what He brought you out of. He loves you. He *loves* you. He has a plan for your life. You've come this far... everything you've endured... all the pain... all the sacrifices... Let it go! Today is the day!" And then he said, *"You are the apple of His eye!"* It hit me—my lawyer said those very words! The lawyer said, "You must be the apple of His eye!"

At that point, my body started to shake. Amy was looking at me and I had tears streaming down my face. I was looking up and sobbing. That's when I knew God was speaking to me. I knew God saw me. He really sees me. He loves me. He knows I exist. He really loves me.

And the man continued. He preached the Gospel of forgiveness. "It doesn't matter how many times you hurt Him; God will never stop loving you. He'll never let you go. He brought you here to this point. When will you realize that He is enough for you?"

Pastor Kinson said, "Do you want to pray? Or do you need someone to pray for you? Come forward! Come forward and someone will pray with you right now." I looked at Amy, and she already knew. She was already putting her hands on me. She was already rejoicing. *She was already thanking God!*

She already knew that I had—right there—let myself open up. She knew my soul was bare, and I was exposed for who I was, in front of God. She wasn't praying for me, saying, "Lord, save her." No! She was already thanking God because He had already saved me! She had her hands up and she was rejoicing, and I was sobbing. I was hysterical. I did not care about how I looked. I didn't care. It felt so good. I felt the freedom!

It felt like my whole body was on fire. It felt… I know it's going to sound cheesy… it felt like my whole heart was getting stitched back together. I felt new; my body was tingling all over. Everything in me wanted to collapse, but I went to the altar. When we were done praying, I got up, and I looked at Amy and we hugged. I remember when we walked up the aisle to go outside; I was wobbly, but I felt like I was on cloud nine! I had this smile on my face that I don't remember I ever wore before.

It was time to leave. On the way to the door, Pastor Kinson was waiting by the door, and he said to me, "It's so good that you came today. I *know* you'll be back!"

It's as though this man was praying for me already. And he said it. He said, "I'll be praying for you." And I know he was.

I went outside and right away I noticed the night sky. I thought, *Wow! The stars are beautiful! They are the most beautiful thing I've ever seen!* I went home that night ecstatic. I knew I was a whole new person.

But when I got home, I was greeted with a lot of hostility. There was fighting between the people I was staying with and their daughter. The daughter was ready to go. She told me she was going to run away.

I had just come from church a few minutes before. I had just had this amazing moment. I felt so happy, and to come home to this? I felt so angry all over again. I wanted to say, *How dare you?*

I had made friends with the woman across the street. So, when the daughter said she wanted to get some fresh air. I suggested a diversion "Let's go across the street. Let's go talk to her and see how she's doing."

The first thing she greeted me with was a joint of marijuana.

"No. No, thanks. I'm good."

She looked at me, surprised that I wasn't interested. "Oh. Okay. Well, what happened with you?"

"I'm okay. I'm good. I don't want to get high. I don't want to drink. I don't want to do anything."

When I got back to the house, the parents told me I had to leave. That I was a bad influence on their daughter. That I was making her worse than what she was. I know it was the devil that was influencing them. But see how good God is.

It was the devil in all the anger when I got there, and he wanted to steal my joy. But I believe God was in that they kicked me out because the minute they kicked me out, I called Amy.

"Amy, I've got nowhere to go. I got here tonight, and they kicked me out."

"Don't worry about it. Just pray. Just pray now."

I got off the phone, and I thought, *Praying? That's your answer—praying? Why doesn't anybody want to help me?*

I was angry. But then it hit me that she gave good advice. I decided I was going to be quiet, and I was going to pray. And that's it. I laid there, and I prayed. And I prayed. And I prayed. I didn't even know how to pray, but I was repeating the same thing over and over again.

Please help me. Please help me, God. Please help me, please.

Amy called back. She had spoken with one of the pastors. He knew of one of the elder women from the church who was a single woman living by herself. He thought she would appreciate it if I came to stay with her.

It was immediate. My heart was jumping for joy.

Is this it? Is this the time of my life where I can serve You now, God? Because I want to serve You. I don't want to go back to the streets. I don't want to go back to a life of crime. I want to serve You.

The next day, they came and picked me up. I said goodbye to the family, and I thanked them so much for having me. I got in the car, and we drove to the woman's house. Her name was Shari. I stayed with Shari through the rest of my probation.

⌘

After I moved in with Shari, I started going to church frequently. I also joined women's prayer meetings. I started getting in tune with God and experiencing His presence. I could hear Him and feel Him.

My relationship with God had gotten so good because I wanted to spend time with Him, and Shari was teaching me that. She was being my spiritual mother. She was teaching me things that would keep my relationship with God alive. We're not as disciplined as we need to be. So, she taught me how to establish the good habits that we need as Christians: To read, in order to feed my spirit daily. To fast. To praise Him. To seek His presence.

To come to Him with an empty heart. This was an important lesson. We don't easily open ourselves to be healed. We don't open ourselves to be completely how God wants us to be in His presence. He wants us to be ourselves with all the rawness of our souls and our spirit. He wants us to expose who we really are and what we're really battling with.

I want to go to God with an empty heart so that He can fill it. It's not full. It's never full enough. I'm so hungry all the time for Him. So, I want to go to Him an empty heart. I want Him to fill it. I want Him to come inside my heart and heal everything so that I can recuperate from the inside out.

I learned that it's human nature to want to cover up our faults and insecurities with a mask. I can go to God and I can recite all this scripture like I already know everything.

But God knows our real pain. He understands our struggles and what we're going through. Even the mental things that we don't tell anyone out loud. So, when I approach Him and I'm wearing my mask, He calls me out. "You're not talking about what's *really* bothering you."

He doesn't want us to go to Him with what we already know. *God, I'm in Your presence again. I'm praying again. I'm reading again. I'm in the same spot. I know You're going to bless me.*

God wants us to come to Him with those secret things. He wants us to come to Him with things we are battling with.

The habits like this were what she taught me. I began to grow in my spirituality. I felt like God was calling me to do something for His kingdom. I enrolled in seminary school. I earned my associate's degree in theological studies and the science of religion.

Then God opened a door for me to come back to my family in Pennsylvania. I was off probation and everything was great.

And I was free.

I continued my studies until I earned my master's degree. I began visiting different churches, telling my testimony to let people know what God had done in my life. I do this because God is so real and very much alive. And He still is in the business of saving lives.

He will change your life if you allow it.

Sioni

"I am here to learn from you guys."

I let the class know that we always learn from each other.

"Just because I'm sitting over here doesn't mean that I think I'm better than you or that I have it all together. That's not how I am. I'm here to learn from you. If anything, you guys encourage me to go on with my life and to not complain about unimportant things."

Many of the women in class encourage me! They say, "You know, Sioni, we're here for you." There is a bond.

About three years ago, I met an inmate who was a psychologist. The irony in this was that she had a degree in psychology, and her specialty was to work with drug abusers. And she had been convicted for drug abuse.

I noticed the way that she kept herself, even in her brown jumpsuit. She didn't say much, but I could tell by the way she spoke that she was well educated. She sat quietly, listening to me. Toward the end, she said, "Thank you for coming." I said, "Oh, no, thank you for being in the class!"

The following Sunday, she came to the class again. I noticed that she had become like a mom to a lot of the inmates. It's not unusual for the younger inmates to connect with older ladies this way. I was talking to the class when she raised her hand to speak. "You know what? I'm coming to your class, but I don't actually believe in God. Still, I come to your class because I like to hear what you have to say. You are a great encourager to me. I want to thank you so much."

She went on to say, "I have a degree in psychology." I know I looked shocked. My eyes *must have opened wide because the girls laughed at me.*

Drugs don't care about the person. Drugs can attack any human being. It doesn't matter your social status or how much money you make. Drugs don't have respect for anyone.

This woman started coming to the class regularly. She came because she felt that what I brought to these women is what they needed to hear.

I encourage them to do better. I try to bring ideas that they can use to help them get through their day. I tell them, "You know what? You are someone. You can change your life. There is great potential for your life!"

She started saying some things that were pretty impressive to me. I decided to ask her to talk to the group about a subject that wasn't in my materials: self-esteem. She was able to immediately start talking about it, and it was very impressive.

She kept coming to the class until she was released. In the end, I said, "Thank you so much for sharing these things. I took lots of notes myself and now you're encouraging me!"

⌘

I first met Elena about four years ago. She was very quiet, but she paid close attention to the class discussion. She was smart and curious to learn new things. She always brought her Bible and a journal she would write in. She would often show me pictures of her children. She had a beautiful smile, especially when she spoke of them.

She was always writing things down, so I had her take attendance and write the class discussion notes. She was always very thorough. If the inmates said, "I want you to pray for me," she would write down every detail.

Elena had a special gift—she wrote lovely poetry. She would offer to read her poems aloud to me, and sometimes to the class. Some were upbeat, some not so much. It all depended on her mood on the day she wrote them. But the subject would be about things that happen in life.

I heard from her after her release, about a year ago. I immediately called her back.

"Let's get together! Where do you live now?"

It happened that she lived only about five minutes away from where I work. I was excited about her being so nearby.

"How about if we get together! We can meet and have lunch so that I can see how you're doing."

I drove from my job on my lunch hour to meet her at a restaurant. She had three beautiful children. Her two daughters were aged 5 and 3, and her son was 10 years old. Her children were very well behaved.

It was so nice to see her again! She said, "I've got a beat-up car, but it's my uncle's car that he's lending me to do my rounds while I'm looking for a job." I could see that she wanted to do right with her life.

When our lunches arrived, she divided her order between the three children. It was so nice to see the tender care of this mother for her children. I met her when she was a girl. She still had that beautiful smile. But now I can see how she has changed into a woman and an attentive mother.

We took some pictures. It was like a family reunion to be able to spend time with her children. We talked, and she told me all the things she wants to do right, like looking for a job. A couple of days later she let me know that she was working at a coffee shop.

Elena gives me hope that it's the right thing to visit these women in prison. When she was incarcerated, she told me, "Sioni, I'm going to change. I'm going to do right by my children."

And that's exactly what she's doing. Now she knows her purpose.

I haven't seen her back at the prison, and I don't expect to. Occasionally I see her post on social media. It's usually something about the kids, going to the park in summer or whatever they're doing.

People can change their circumstances. Second chances are real.

" 10 "

SECOND CHANCES

I met Audrey when she was only 17 years old. She was especially beautiful. And she was being held in maximum security.

Her boyfriend ran drugs and she was caught with him when he was arrested. Her boyfriend is doing twenty-five years, and she was doing ten. They charged her as an adult, even though she was underage.

Audrey was in maximum security for two years before she was sent to another state prison. After she left, we began exchanging letters each month. We wrote to each other for four years, and I accumulated a tall stack of letters from her. She confided to me in her letters about how difficult life in prison was for her.

> "Dear Sioni... I've been struggling a lot here. I just want to go home. I don't really get along with anyone in this program and it's really hard to stay in the word and follow God being here. I don't know. I've been in a rut almost and it's hard to get out of it. I've been worried about my boyfriend a lot and don't know what to do about it. I just feel like giving up sometimes."

I also communicated with her mother and I would ask her how Audrey was doing. She told me that she wasn't doing very well. Audrey didn't like where she was because she was with the general population.

I went to see her even though she was about two hours from my house. It was Christmastime when Richard and I visited. This was the first time I was able to see her since she had been transferred seven months before.

When you go to visit a prisoner, you begin by obtaining clearance to see the inmate. You'll stay in a small waiting room at first, and then will be moved to a large community room. There are chairs from end to end, and all visitors and family come to the same room.

You can buy the inmate whatever they want in the vending machines they have there. There's a *yellow line before you get to the vending machines. They have to stay behind that yellow line, point out to you what they want, and then you go and get it for them. They are not allowed to touch the vending machines.*

The officers are set up high where they can see the entire room at once. Soon after Richard and I arrived in this room, I saw Audrey coming out, down the steps towards us. She was so excited that she jumped down the two steps, calling out my name, "Sioni! Sioni!" I felt like my heart was going to come out of my chest because I was so happy. Audrey was one of my girls, and a lot of them had moved to a different state prison. But Audrey was the only one that had stayed connected.

I asked her if she wanted something from the machines. She wanted a diet soda, cookies, and some chips. And then we talked. She described what it was like and how she didn't like it there, but that she had faith in God that things would get better. Then she told me she was going to school, and she was getting her degree as a graphic designer. I was so happy to hear her speak about her goals.

My husband and I were there for about an hour. And then I saw dogs and asked what they were doing there. She explained that they bring the dogs in to bring comfort to the inmates. I thought that was pretty cool.

We were allowed to take pictures with the inmates, and we posed for several. Later she sent me a postcard with a picture of her with a dog beside her. Audrey is a very sweet girl.

After the visit, we continued writing each other letters. Her moods in the letters were very up and down. In the beginning, she described how she was starting not to want to deal with God anymore. She felt that God was not there for her. She thought that God had abandoned her. She was feeling like all the things that were happening to her were because God wasn't with her.

I wrote her back to let her know that God would never leave her, that God has a plan in her life. Sometimes we do things in life where we have to pay the consequence.

"Hello, Audrey... I got your pictures. You look so beautiful! My husband and I were so happy to see you again. We are so proud of you, to hear about all the things that you have in mind and the future for you. Remember to always put God first. He will order your path. We want to encourage you, for we know you are feeling down. Give your burdens to the Lord, for it's there that love is found. We just want you to know, we're praying that the Lord will touch you right where you are, with the *peace you're longing for. I pray for you today that God will touch your life, that you may know more and more each day."*

At first, she didn't understand. Audrey was young, and she was in a place that she wasn't familiar with, and she didn't like the changes. She told me she didn't know what to do with her boyfriend. I didn't want to tell her to leave him because that was not my place. But I did tell her that "I think God has something better for you in your life." I didn't tell her that she'd better leave him because he was going to be incarcerated for so many years. But I wanted her to come out and be able to do something good for her life.

How could she expect to stay together with him while he would be in jail for 25 years? That's how those young girls think sometimes. They don't see their future. They live in the moment.

I received about thirty letters from Audrey. And in every letter, she would mention her ups and downs, how she didn't like to be there. But in the last year or two, the letters were becoming more confident about the things happening in her life. She was able to get a job in jail. She got a degree while she was incarcerated. She's working hard to do right for herself.

"Dear Sioni... I've been doing a lot better. Still struggling, but better. Being in a new place isn't always easy for me. It took me a while to get used to it but now I'm getting into a routine. God has given me more of an understanding of my purpose and about Himself. I know that God is moving and working even though I can't always see it or understand it."

Sometimes she worries and I tell her, "Audrey, you know you have no control over what happens on the outside. Even though you want to help, you can't. You've got to ask God to guide you in the decisions you have to make."

Her mother and I keep in touch. Whenever I call and ask how Audrey's doing, she says that she's doing much better.

Audrey has already made the decision on where to live after she's released. As much as she wants to be with her mom, she knows that the best thing she could do would be to move in with her Grandmother. If she lives there, she'll be able to start over in a new environment. I hope that she'll visit our church from time to time. If she came for the day, we could get together and have lunch, and just talk.

Audrey's mother lives about two hours away and I've never met her. She's very supportive of Audrey. She's pretty incredible, actually. Her mother goes to see her at least twice a week. Apparently, both of Audrey's parents are very supportive of her. It makes me think that she's not going to have to do this on her own.

Many inmates go to jail and their families don't make the effort to reach out to them. Sometimes they don't even care about them. Fortunately for Audrey, her family is very connected to her. This support is vital to all of us, but especially so for an inmate.

Audrey's most recent letter came with the wonderful news that she's up for parole very soon!

I wrote back, excited to be able to encourage her further.

"Dear Audrey... You know when you get out, you're starting a new season. Your life is going to change. It's good that you're going to be living with your grandmother. Your grandmother is a believer and will bring you to church. And while you're in the church, try to do things for God."

She's understandably excited. She's looking forward to what God has in store for her. She's looking out to find a job.

I'm excited about what God's got planned for her. I'll be a witness for that because she'll be living close by. Once she gets out, I'll meet up with her and we'll have a lunch celebration. That will be a beautiful thing. Imagine it!

When I first met her, Audrey was very quiet and kept to herself most of the time. But lately, she tells me that she smiles a lot more; now she talks more. I can see from her letters to me, that she's reaching out to other women. I believe she has become the leader of the women in there. Without a support system, she might not be brave enough to do that.

And best of all, she knows the Word.

"Dear Audrey… It is so good to hear from you. You say that you are working now, and that is wonderful news. I am so happy to hear that and happy for you.

"Always remember: God has a purpose for each of our lives. Sometimes, we don't see the light at the end of the tunnel. But, in all the darkness we can still see the hand of God. We can take His hand and run to the end of the tunnel because what He has waiting for us outside will be ever so much better."

Audrey is finally out of prison, has a job, and is doing well for herself.

⌘

Cora messaged me this morning to tell me she's going to have a baby.

I met Cora about two years ago in a unit on the east side of the prison. The first time I met Cora I was there with Richard. We went to that unit first, from 1:30 to 2:30 in the afternoon.

We were given a large room to use. The first thing that we did was to set up two long, brown folding tables and plastic chairs all around. The chairs are all different colors: blue and beige and tan. Through the glass, you can see the courtyard. The courtyard isn't outside, though. It's an inside room. But this is where the girls play basketball or take walks.

When we were done setting up the tables, the girls started coming in. It gets pretty crowded sometimes, so I always offer my chair but of course, they don't want it. They prefer sometimes to stand up, but we always find enough chairs around. After we were all sitting, I remember looking at every girl. I don't know all their names, all the time, but I do know their faces.

This one particular girl came and sat down beside me. I looked at her and thought she was quite beautiful. She's a young-looking girl with curly light brown hair and green eyes and birthmarks on her cheeks. She seemed very sweet when we said hello to each other.

I introduced myself to the group and had them introduce themselves. I went around the room, as I always do, and asked each one—from one to ten, with ten being the high number—how they felt that day. Then I told them a joke as a way to break the ice.

When I present the Gospel, I try to talk about things that could happen in modern-day situations. Sometimes I tell stories about women in the Bible. Whatever the day's subject, my goal is always to bring hope, encouragement, and joy. I find out what they need to hear about, and then I bring it to them.

Cora was beside me, and I could see that she was taking notes. She had a Bible, and she asked me if she could use my highlighter to mark passages in her Bible.

The next time I came it was the same kind of thing. We did that twice a month. I stopped seeing her for a while until one day I saw her upstairs. She was in a different unit than the one I go to. This time I wasn't with Richard, but by myself.

This unit is different, and the girls have to sign up for a special program to be allowed there. It's a more comfortable unit, almost cozy. Well, cozy for jail, anyway. The inmates are there to show that they are going to be able to do the right things when they are released.

I talked to Cora, and she shared with me that she has two daughters. One was almost 14 at that time and the other is younger. She participated with the group, but I noticed that she was happy some days, and very sad on other days.

Eventually, she was released from prison. When the girls in my class leave, sometimes they try to contact me. Sometimes they leave and they don't contact me at all. One day I got an electronic message from Cora. She said, "Hey Sioni, it's me." I wasn't sure who it was at first. Then I saw her picture, and I was very happy to hear from her.

"I'm not sure if you remember me, but I remember you when you used to come to the jail," she said. "When I was able to share with you, you made such a big impact on my life." She continued, "You're a strong woman. I pray to God that He gives me the knowledge and the strength to overcome things the way He did for you."

I wanted to get together with her to catch up, but she had moved away to live with her Aunt Eugenia in another state. We chatted for a while. Her news was as good as I could hope for.

"I'm doing good. I'm changing. I'm not the same as I was." She let me know that she met someone, and they were in love.

"Life is getting better. I'm getting married. Now I have all my kids back with me. My life is changing, and I have wonderful things in my life."

Then a couple of months later, she sent me another letter, and it was my wedding invitation. I was so happy! Of course, I didn't think I knew her personally enough to go to her wedding. And she had assured me that she understood that it might be too difficult for us to attend. After all, the wedding was almost six hours away.

Still, I told Richard, "I feel like God wants me to go to this wedding. I feel like I need to be there to support her." And Richard said, "Absolutely. We will definitely go."

She said, "I'm so excited I can't wait to see you. It's been a long journey from the prison to here. You were such a huge part of the reason I've become the Christian woman I am today. And when I was making my wedding invitations, I knew I wanted you to be there."

I was so excited to be going that I started planning right away for the trip. I made the arrangements for the hotel and the car rental. I bought her a gift and, I shopped for new shoes and a dress for the wedding.

We left on Friday after finishing work and arrived at our hotel around 1 A.M. on Saturday morning. But we were up and getting ready after some sleep and left for the church and the wedding.

I didn't know this, but in that area in that particular town that we were in, the houses were very close to each other. It was sweet. It was like an alley, not like a normal street. It was like little streets around the houses. And the houses were very small houses, and they were close to each other. And then you go up all the way up into the mountain and then you're coming down. It was like being in a Pac-Man machine.

Richard and I were driving around and getting a little irritated. It was getting late, and we were not finding the church. I called ahead to say we were running late. The bride was unfazed. She said, "Calm down. It's going to be fine, everything's going to be fine."

We finally made our way to the church. As we wound into the driveway, we saw there was no one outside. But as we were pulling in to park, I saw the bride. She was outside with someone else, but as she saw us pull in, she started crying. Richard urged me to go to her. "Honey, run, run! Look at her—she's crying because she sees you!"

It was pretty emotional. She was crying. She was patting her face and dabbing her eyes. I didn't want her to ruin her make-up. I didn't want to ruin my makeup either! I said, "Don't cry!" I held her so tight. It gave me such a beautiful feeling because I hadn't seen her for two years.

She looked so healthy now. She had lost some weight. She had such a glowing face. And she looked so beautiful with her white gown. It was not floor length, but it was almost down to her ankles. She had her veil down to a bit past her shoulders. Her dress had a 1960s look to it. The top of her dress had sequins and beads. It was beautiful.

She introduced me to her family and to the pastor who was going to perform the ceremony. She held us back from taking our seats right away. She said, "Stay with us for this. I'd love for you to be in the room as the pastor prays for me."

We came together with her family and we started to pray. She told everybody in the room, "This woman who is here... she came into my life when I was at my lowest point." That meant so much to me. There have been many times when I left the prison wondering if I made any difference at all. Did they get anything from me today? Anything?

But when Cora was talking about me, I knew that it was all worth it because she did get it. She continued, "You were there to speak Life to me."

I remember her in our group at the prison. I remember seeing her wandering around the table with her eyes while I was talking. Maybe she wasn't making eye contact, but the whole time she was listening to everything.

We hadn't met the groom yet because all this was happening in the back of the church. The groom was at the front of the church waiting for the bride to walk down the aisle. He was wearing a suit, and he looked very nice, too.

We were looking at the front of the church at the pastor and the groom and I saw a little girl throwing flowers. I found out later that the flower girl was Cora's daughter, and she was about seven or eight years old. The music began, and the bride started coming down the aisle. She was glowing, emotional, and happy. She walked in and they exchanged their vows and it was simply beautiful.

Her sixteen-year-old daughter and some other family members couldn't be there. So, they recorded messages that were shown on TV screens that had been set up. It was a way to have all the family members participate, even if they couldn't attend in person. The message from her daughter was bittersweet but lovely.

They had five tables on each side of the room for the reception. They were set with red tablecloths, and centerpieces decorated in black and gold. Several people spoke and congratulated the couple. Cora asked me to go to the front to say a few words.

I looked at her. I looked at her family. I started by introducing myself. I explained that I had met Cora about two years ago.

I remembered Cora in her darkest places.

"But look at her today. I believe in second chances. I believe that God can change people."

I made eye contact with her aunt who was sobbing quietly. There were tears in the eyes of others as well. It was as if they were only now realizing how far Cora had come. And that she really could change.

"People change. Sometimes we lose hope, but God doesn't lose His hope in us. We know this from Jeremiah 29:11." I recited the quote.

> **"For I know the plans I have for you," declares the Lord, "plans to prosper you and not to harm you, plans to give you hope and a future."**
> Jeremiah 29:11 (NIV)

I like her husband. He appears to be a very humble man. They met when he was working for her uncle. It took them a little while to start dating, but Cora got her second chance.

Cora came and sat down, and we spoke a bit.

"Sioni, today is the day that marks two years since I've used any kind of drugs in my life."

Choosing this date to be married will create double the reason to celebrate each year. She'll be celebrating her sobriety and her wedding at the same time!

I was going for seconds. I said, "Cora, the food is so good!"

She said, "I cooked it!"

"Cora—you did everything for your wedding?"

"Yes, I did, Sioni."

I was so proud of her. "It's your day, and here you cook your own food for your guests! That was so good! So nice!"

After that we took pictures, and we said goodbye to everyone. We went back to the hotel and stayed overnight. We left on Sunday.

Recently she sent me a message. She was overjoyed when she told me her news.

"Have you heard yet? I'm pregnant!"

Her happy ending has only just begun!

⌘

My commitment to God cannot be shaken. His commitment to us cannot be denied. So, if God finds value in all of us, then I must honor the value of all people, no matter how lost they may seem. For God, there is no person without potential.

These are statements that I live by. They have proven to be true in my life, and they can be true for you, as well. I share them with you now, to encourage you to adopt them as your own!

I believe in second chances.

I believe everyone deserves a second chance.

I believe people can and do change.

I believe that God has a purpose for each and every one of us.

And, I believe with all my heart, that if we are still here,

it is because God is not yet finished with us.

Father God allow our lives to demonstrate how You will never abandon us. Let the world know peace through
Your Saving Grace!

AFTERWORD

Scheila

To you who are *not* incarcerated...

I believe that the devil is purposefully manipulating situations for evil. The result is the incarceration of people who have some of the highest potential to live in God's purpose. Once captured, they won't be able to shine their light out to the rest of the world.

But these people have great value to the Lord. Jesus charges us with visiting those who are in jail and listening to the downtrodden. The Bible shows how He says it in different ways over and over and over and over again.

Our purpose is to provide guidance and nurturance that inmates need to succeed. That way, when they are released into society, they can be the Warriors that they were always meant to be.

We already know they are warriors. In order for you to survive incarceration, you have to be a fighter. You have to be somebody who's willing to wake up every day and keep going because if you don't, you'll die mentally. You'll die physically. You'll die because in the long run there's no one there to breathe life into you.

We work to change the mindset of the incarcerated. They change from warriors *for* the darkness to warriors *against* the darkness.

I believe that God picked this time for me. Now as a free woman—and with my relationship to Him—I can explain the need to others. I say, "Hey, let's not turn our backs on people who are incarcerated. Don't look at it as somebody who cannot be reformed. Don't look at somebody who has a prior record as if he can't do something for the Kingdom of God. Because we can. We all have a purpose. God can use anyone, at any time, with the abilities that God chooses to send them."

Our job is not to reach only those that we're comfortable with. We've got to get our hands dirty sometimes. That's okay if that's part of saving a soul. That's our job. As Christians, it's our job to reach deep down to those who are the lowest, the down-and-out. *That's our job.*

I want people to develop a place of compassion, where they can understand, "it could be me." It could be you. It could be your kid. It could be anybody. Either today or tomorrow they make a bad decision, or they're in the wrong place at the wrong time. People are getting incarcerated today for no reason. You could end up with somebody that you love dearly, who is incarcerated.

Is it okay to wait to reach out until there's somebody that you know who's incarcerated? Sure. But there are people there now that you don't know, who need somebody to reach them. They need somebody to go there now to give them hope and tell them about second chances. People can find a spot in their hearts for the incarcerated. A place where they understand that there's somebody in there right now that they could reach out to. That these people are worthy. And all of us are capable of being used by God to reach them.

To you who are incarcerated now...

Sometimes it's going to seem like God isn't listening. Prepare yourself for this so that you'll know what to do when it happens to you.

Fight. Keep fighting.

There are many walls and many obstacles. It's not easy. Nothing is ever easy. It's never going to be easy. The hardest thing you've faced in life will seem like one of the easiest things, compared to what you'll have to overcome in being a Christian.

Being a Christian is not for the faint of heart. Being a Christian is not for the weak-minded. Being filled with faith and hope is not for someone who is going to throw in the towel easily.

It's a dedication and a commitment you have to make every day. It is breaking down walls—walls that *you* have placed there for years. Walls that *you* have made so thick that you have to punch through until you're raw-knuckled. And keep punching until you can't feel the pain anymore.

There are going to be things that you're going to have to overcome and it's going to feel like God is a million miles away. And that's part of it. That's part of overcoming the world to feel true faith. To find true hope, to really feel God, you must understand what to do when you feel like there's no one there sometimes. And know that it's okay. That's part of it.

But He's always there. He's always been there from the beginning. When you didn't feel Him before, He was there. So, don't doubt now. If you felt God even once, you know what He's capable of doing. You know God is capable of saving you.

And if you've experienced that, hold on to that. Hold fast onto what He's going to do for you. He's already promised.

He's already promised in His word what He has for you. You already know who you are.

You've been sanctified. You've been redeemed. You've been set apart.

You are His daughter. You are His princess. You are a future queen.

There's no reason why you can't keep fighting. Don't give up.

Just keep fighting. You'll be there. And I'll be there praying with you. And you have sisters and brothers and a whole kingdom that is behind you.

And God is standing there, and He's telling you, "Just keep going."

Just keep going.

You've got to train before you go out to the race. The Bible tells us, *Prepare.* Go out there. Fight. Keep fighting. Paul said, "Run the good race that has been set before you." It's serious stuff and you have to be a warrior. And whatever you've had to do in life that you overcame, you can overcome this, too. In God, now.

Now you have the power you need. Keep fighting.

You've been used to fighting your whole life. Now it's a serious time. This is not a street-level brawl. Now you're getting in the ring with the knockout king. You're getting in the ring with the devil. You've got to prepare yourself. You've got to know 100%. You've got to be confident in your faith.

And understand that it's going to require you to go through some serious things. But when you go through them... *praise God...* you're going to see the outcome. And you're going to realize... *glory be to God...* that everything you went through was for a reason.

So, praise God. And keep fighting

ABOUT THE AUTHORS

Sioni Rodriguez is the author of the book, THREE TIMES SOLD, a story of overcoming a childhood of unrelenting abuse, the faith that saved her, and the forgiveness that brought her peace. She advocates for other survivors as an ambassador for Project Rescue and as a team member with *A Time To Heal Beyond Survival International Ministries.*

She is also committed to ministering to incarcerated women. She helps them find their own true value, and the hope they need to build lives beyond the prison walls.

She is available as a motivational speaker for churches, conferences, and other events, both internationally and in the United States.

Reach her by email to: *srwestpointmom@gmail.com.*

Scheila Singley is the first woman that her mother, Sioni, helped to overcome the miserable existence resulting from doing time in prison.

Growing from life on the streets to a spark of hope of a better way, to a full-blown revival, Scheila has since earned a master's degree in theology and is noa devoted wife and mother.

Reach her by email to: *singleyscheila@yahoo.com.*

Sioni's Personal Story of Faith, Survival and Forgiveness

Raised in poverty under unthinkable conditions, she might have been lost to a life of pain and abuse. This was almost guaranteed when, as a young girl, she was sold into bondage—a young victim of human trafficking. Instead, she escaped and created a new life for herself. It wasn't easy. She worked hard and overcame the troubles that threatened to crush her.

Available in Paperback and Kindle from Amazon.com.

Made in the USA
Monee, IL
02 March 2021